AMERICAN BLOODS

AMERICAN
BLOODS

★ ★ ★ ★ ★ ★ ★ ★ ★ ★ ★ ★ ★

The Untamed Dynasty
That Shaped a Nation

JOHN KAAG

FARRAR, STRAUS AND GIROUX
NEW YORK

Farrar, Straus and Giroux
120 Broadway, New York 10271

Illustration credits can be found on pages 269–270.

Library of Congress Cataloging-in-Publication Data
Names: Kaag, John, 1979– author.
Title: American Bloods : the untamed dynasty that shaped a nation / John Kaag.
Description: First edition. | New York : Farrar, Straus and Giroux, 2024. |
    Includes bibliographical references and index.
Identifiers: LCCN 2023051085 | ISBN 9780374103910 (hardcover)
Subjects: LCSH: Blood family. | Blood, Robert, 1628–1701—Family. | Blood,
    Thaddeus, 1755–1844—Family. | Blood, Thaddeus, 1755–1844—Homes and
    haunts. | Massachusetts—Biography. | New England—Biography.
Classification: LCC CS71.B655 2024 | DDC 929.20973—dc23/eng/20231102
LC record available at https://lccn.loc.gov/2023051085

Designed by Patrice Sheridan

Our books may be purchased in bulk for promotional, educational, or business
use. Please contact your local bookseller or the Macmillan Corporate and
Premium Sales Department at 1-800-221-7945, extension 5442, or by email at
MacmillanSpecialMarkets@macmillan.com.

www.fsgbooks.com
Follow us on social media at @fsgbooks

1   2   3   4   5   6   7   8   9   10

For Kathleen

In wildness is the preservation of the world.

—HENRY DAVID THOREAU, "WALKING"
(CONCEIVED ON A WALK TO VISIT PEREZ BLOOD)

We need the tonic of wildness . . . At the same time that we are earnest to explore and learn all things, we require that all things be mysterious and unexplorable, that land and sea be infinitely wild, unsurveyed and unfathomed by us because unfathomable.

—HENRY DAVID THOREAU, *WALDEN*
(WRITTEN THREE MILES FROM BLOOD FARM)

CONTENTS

BLOOD FAMILY TREE

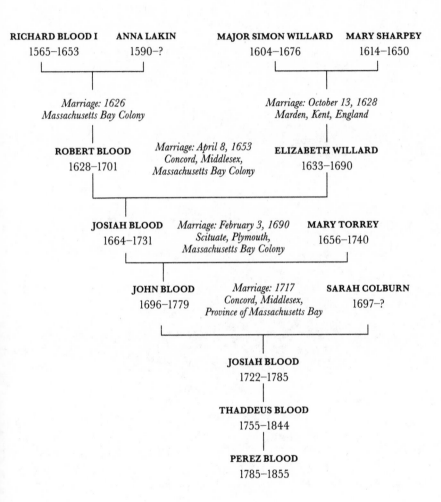

RICHARD BLOOD I
1565–1653

ANNA LAKIN
1590–?

MAJOR SIMON WILLARD
1604–1676

MARY SHARPEY
1614–1650

Marriage: 1626
Massachusetts Bay Colony

Marriage: October 13, 1628
Marden, Kent, England

ROBERT BLOOD
1628–1701

Marriage: April 8, 1653
Concord, Middlesex,
Massachusetts Bay Colony

ELIZABETH WILLARD
1633–1690

JOSIAH BLOOD
1664–1731

Marriage: February 3, 1690
Scituate, Plymouth,
Massachusetts Bay Colony

MARY TORREY
1656–1740

JOHN BLOOD
1696–1779

Marriage: 1717
Concord, Middlesex,
Province of Massachusetts Bay

SARAH COLBURN
1697–?

JOSIAH BLOOD
1722–1785

THADDEUS BLOOD
1755–1844

PEREZ BLOOD
1785–1855

AMERICAN BLOODS

PROLOGUE: THE WOLF ≡

A she-wolf was at his heels, who in her leanness
seemed full of all wants . . .

—DANTE ALIGHIERI, *INFERNO*, 1308[1]

I SAW IT FIRST IN THE FADING LIGHT OF A NOVEM-
ber afternoon, standing at the corner of a meadow of the Great
Brook, on the edge of the forest, a hundred yards away. A dog
that had slipped its collar. Moments later, I saw it again, closer
this time: a large dog, a husky perhaps, moving slowly and quietly in an outcropping of gray birch.

Even in broad daylight, dogs are not my favorite animals.
Many years ago, I witnessed a sheepdog—a gentle creature that
had been bred to protect the gentlest—maul a boy's face beyond
recognition, and that had been enough to make me quietly ter-
rified of man's best friend: clearly, domestication only goes so
far. So when I go running in the evening, I usually carry a stick
just for occasions like this one. But tonight, in my hurry to get
out the door, I'd forgotten it. I was two miles from our house, a
weathered, whitewashed colonial farmhouse on the outskirts of
Carlisle, Massachusetts, whose warm lights peek comfortingly
through Tophet Swamp.

I considered making a dash for it, but that would involve crossing the wetland, and I didn't relish racing a hound through the shadows. Besides, I knew that running was self-defeating, that I should pull myself together, stop, and calmly face the animal. It was, after all, someone's pet. A sizable one, but still a pet. It probably was lost. At the edge of the darkness, I slowed my pace and looked back.

As it emerged from the cluster of trees, one thing became certain: this definitely was not a dog. Or even a coyote. Its broad, distinctive head bobbed toward me, and I remember making a sound—guttural and primal—that was somewhere between a scream and a howl. The wolf stopped and sat on its haunches. Then it turned and bounded away through the brush, its thick gray tail streaming behind. Within seconds, it was gone, but that scarcely mattered. Bolting into Tophet Swamp, I ran directly through the frozen muck, toward the safety of home.

In the Bible, "Tophet" means "hell." There are a dozen Tophet Swamps in Massachusetts. Spaced exactly ten miles apart, they create a more or less direct route from the interior of the state to Salem, waylays along what was once the Mohawk Trail. When the Puritans arrived in America, they needed a word to describe unwelcome places that could not be tamed—otherworldly, dangerous places where people often lost their way or, worse, their lives. According to Genesis, Tophet was a site in the Valley of Hinnom where the Canaanites would burn their children alive. Only the sounds of drums and tambourines could drown out the screams of the innocent. So in the early days of colonial America, "Tophet" came to describe anything unspeakably frightening, a lair of wild beasts, say, but also the holy ground of the Native peoples the Europeans encountered.

The sachems who led the five tribes that lived in what would become Massachusetts were drawn to the wetlands—their seclusion, their phosphorescent gases that glowed at night, their primordial, wild nature.

In my flight, I'd given up any attempt to find an actual trail through the swamp and was careening through the trees in near darkness, guided only by the little porch lantern from the farmhouse adjacent to our own. Lone wolves come in two varieties: aging females who are abandoned by or driven from their pack, and ambitious young males in search of more territory. Wolves hunt in coordinated groups, preying on large animals like deer. A single wolf doesn't stand much of a chance of catching one. So lone wolves are usually hungry. They feed on carrion, or they hunt smaller, weaker, slower animals. My sneakers were coated with a thick mud that made running nearly impossible. But run I did, until I didn't. A black mass rose out of the swamp—a set of three oblong granite slabs wedged into the icy ground, propped at angles to form a cave large enough to shelter man or beast. I didn't wait to see what might emerge. I pitched to one side, grabbed a branch to steady myself, and in the process managed to slice my hand and twist my ankle. I hobbled out of the thicket toward civilization.

I COULD SEE the lights of the house next door through the trees.

When I was sixteen, my Latin teacher, Mr. Emes, helped me escape the claustrophobia of my home in Central Pennsylvania. During the summer of my senior year, he took me to Massachusetts, convincing my wary mother that such travel was necessary to my study of the Greeks. What we actually studied on that trip was philosophy—and particularly American transcendentalism, the writings of Henry David Thoreau and Ralph Waldo Emerson. "Trust thyself," Emerson chides, "every heart vibrates to that iron string." We arrived at Walden, on the outskirts of Concord, Massachusetts, in early August and walked around Thoreau's famous pond. At the end of the ramble, I turned to Mr. Emes and announced that I was going to become a philosopher and live in Thoreau's hometown. He just laughed: "Over your mother's dead body." As I write, my mother is still alive. We live not much more than a mile from Walden Pond. I teach philosophy. And I have spent much of my life writing about Thoreau. In 2022, my wife, Kathleen, and I bought an ancient farmhouse on the slopes of the Concord River, at least in part due to its proximity to Walden and Cambridge, quiet, peaceful places suited to contemplation that also happened to be the homes of my intellectual heroes—Thoreau and Emerson but also the American pragmatist William James. Thoreau loved the rolling hills surrounding our house, at one point sauntering through and surveying our yard. Idyllic—that is the word that I used to call this countryside. Until now. The encounter in the Tophet unceremoniously interrupted my life of the mind, which was supposed to be composed at all times.

My daughter Becca, who is now ten—thoughtful, careful, and considerate beyond her years—met me at the side door, looked at my bloody hand and into my eyes.

"What'd you do?" she asked. "What *happened*?"

I wasn't sure what happened. Had I really fled a wolf? Was it dream or reality?

"I'm fine, love, go wash up for dinner."

I changed my clothes, ate some dinner, bathed the kids, and put them to bed—then I told Kath about my run, about the beast, about how our quiet New England village of Carlisle, the sister town of historic Concord, a place so quaintly American it could have been a Norman Rockwell painting come to life, was in fact on the brink of sucking us back into a state of nature. And I told her about the cave of rocks hidden by trees in our own backyard that I'd never noticed until tonight. Kath nodded somberly, patted my leg, and went off into the kitchen.

"You should find another running trail, love. You know that we live on 'the predator superhighway.' That cave has a name. The Bloods called it 'Wolf Rock.'"

I have never been what one might call a superstitious man. I believe that questions, generally speaking, have empirical answers and when such answers are given, we should heed them as best we can. Over the years, however, I've come to believe that certain mysteries of life can neither be answered nor explained away by our rational faculties. When we encounter them, the best we can do is face them quietly in the light of their perplexity. I am absolutely sure I saw a wolf. I am also absolutely sure that this is next to impossible. Whatever it was, I wanted to never see it again. I will tell you some of what I actually know—that does not lead directly to paradox. At one point, the rock I passed that night was, in fact, called Wolf Rock. The rock was set on Blood Farm, a tract of land on the edge of Colonial America. Our house, the refuge on the shores of the river, was owned by Josiah Blood, built in the year of his marriage to Sarah Blood (that was also her maiden name) in 1745. On the evening of my wolf encounter, Kath and I closed up our Blood house, turned the lights out, and headed to bed. It had been a busy day of unpacking, raking, and early holiday shopping. She fell asleep. I did not.

I slipped out of bed, shuffled down the hall without waking the kids, and found myself in front of the massive fireplace in

the Blood living room. Two large cupboards flanked the bee-
hive oven that had been the heart of the home. In the day of
Josiah Blood, a single chimney pulled at five counterpointed
fires throughout the house, just enough, I imagine, to keep the
chill at bay on fall evenings. Winter was probably another story.
The Blood family must have huddled in close and listened to
the wolves. I made a fire of my own, fetched a beer and blanket,
and tried not to think about the swamp behind the house. I
would just have to adjust myself to living in, or at least uncom-
fortably near, the Tophet. We'd very recently purchased the
house, much too recently to consider reselling it.

As the room began to thaw, I moved a large stack of cartons
to be unpacked away from the fireplace. It was after midnight,
but if I worked for an hour, I could probably clear the living
room and make it properly livable by the morning. At least
the inside of the house could appear tamed and well-ordered. I
never got to the unpacking or the cleaning of the cupboard because, as it also turns out, a cupboard is not always a cupboard.
I opened the door and a small room—brick-lined, framed with
black walnut beams—stretched back and slipped into shadows
at the corner of the chimney. There was no need for alarm:
these secret places are not uncommon in colonial farmhouses
from this time. It was totally normal. Houses were usually built
around a central chimney, but the ovens weren't always regularly sized so there was a bit of space that had to be closed off
and remained largely untouched. I knew, even at the time, that
I wasn't being entirely honest with myself. The abnormal part
of the room had nothing to do with the space itself, but everything to do with the ways that the American colonists used
hidden passages like this one. In the early eighteenth century,
they were regularly hiding places for women and children dur-

ing attack, when Native Americans in the region decided that
the settlers had settled on too much of this borderland. In the
coming era, the Underground Railroad would repurpose these
rooms to smuggle formerly enslaved African Americans across
barren northern country to Canada.

I fetched a flashlight and steeled myself. When I was
younger, dark places with forgotten histories didn't frighten me
nearly as much as they should have, but over time and with experience, I've come by a healthier respect for privacy. But this
was *our house*. The room was seven feet deep, four feet across, and
almost completely empty—almost. In the corner of the room
was a lonely chair and on it sat a bag filled with a stack of yellow-
ing paper, an inch thick, bound with a rubber band. I adjusted
my flashlight and made out the cover page:

Privately published by Roger Deane Harris.
THE STORY OF THE BLOODS

As a philosopher and an intellectual historian, I've spent
the better part of my life in old libraries, remote archives, and
forgotten studies. Weird documents and bizarre family genealo-
gies seldom surprise me, but *The Story of the Bloods* was something
else. Sprawling, convoluted, borderline fantastic, riddled with
more than five thousand names, all of them Bloods. "We are
about to take a journey," Harris wrote on the opening page of
his *Story*, "not in distance, but in time back into the happenings
of yesteryear. It is unlikely that many of us will ever actually visit
the many places where these people lived, however it is quite
possible." It is, I was about to find out, imminently possible.[2]

* * *

IN THE SUBSEQUENT days, I combed through *The Story of the Bloods*, and instead of avoiding Wolf Rock, became obsessed with it, skirting it at first, but then climbing it, and finally venturing inside. I remembered Emerson's description of this Tophet: "The country was not yet so thickly settled but that the inhabitants suffered from wolves and wildcats, which infested the woods."

When the Puritans arrived at this place three hundred and fifty years ago, it is said that the wolves greeted them in the twilight, sat on their "tayles," and grinned.[3] In 1648, the Court of Massachusetts decreed that an Englishman who brought a wolf head to the constable should be paid thirty shillings, and "an Indian" who did the same should be paid twenty, ten of which should be given to the constable. In 1661, the reward was adjusted and no mention was made of the head, but the ears of the beast were to be cut off and buried so no hunter could be paid twice for the same carcass. According to early records of the Puritans, wolves were "ravenous cruell creatures and daily vexatious to all ye inhabitants of the Colony."[4] The settlers were cutting down the trees that supported the deer that fed the wolves, but this fact does not seem to have been recorded. The trees were used to build the earliest inland settlements in the American colony, strongholds against the realities of the frontier. At the center of the Massachusetts settlement was the tract of land—half wild, half civilized—upon which our farmhouse now stands, along with a dozen other original colonials. This was Blood Farm, three thousand acres that stretched from present-day Concord north to what is now Carlisle. The Blood family owned it all. It is no exaggeration to say that this is one of the places where the United States grew into itself, with all its excruciating growing pains.

But first, the wolves had to die. In the late 1600s, Robert and John Blood, Josiah's direct ancestors, waged an ongoing and bloody campaign against the wolves and the other native inhabitants of the region. According to legend, John set loose a pack of dogs that hounded the wolves through Tophet Swamp; the wolves either ran north or sought shelter at Wolf Rock.[5] Of course, this "shelter" would ultimately be their grave, the place where a group of weaker animals would corner a lone beast and destroy it. That's one version of the story. The other is that the Rock was the inner citadel of the wolf community, the place where their vicious raids on Concord and Carlisle would originate. It's possible both versions are true; Wolf Rock remains an archetypal American puzzle. Who was its rightful owner, who the vicious invader? Who was the outcast, who the trespasser? What untamed stories lie beneath the skin of our more or less well-functioning society? How persistent is the wildness that once defined our country?

The Blood brothers belonged to one of America's first and most expansive pioneer families, who explored, and laid claim to, the frontiers—geographic, political, intellectual, and spiritual—that became the very core of a nation. Their kin would directly inspire Ralph Waldo Emerson's comment that "America is another name for opportunity," but also awaken in Emerson the sense that great opportunities are the easiest to be squandered. The Bloods embodied the risks and rewards that were taken in laying claim to the lands that would become the United States, a testament to how life, liberty, and happiness are ideas realized in process, honed not in their total fulfillment but in their ongoing, often dangerous and misguided, pursuit. Such ideals live at the edge of things, on the borders of experience, murmuring "ever not quite."

The story of *American Bloods* is not a clean story. It doesn't flow triumphantly to the end. But true stories about places, people, and ideas usually don't. What is supposed to be the most pristine, the realm of pure ideas, is often sullied by human inadequacy and inconsistency. There are, admittedly, more famous "American families"—the Cabots, Lowells, Astors, and Roosevelts. But they aren't the Bloods. The Bloods, unlike many other more visible or iconic American dynasties, consistently, and with remarkable regularity, reveal a particular frontier ethos: their genealogy tracks what Henry David Thoreau called "wildness," an original untamed spirit that would recede in the making of America but never be extinguished entirely. The United States may have been founded on "life, liberty, and the pursuit of happiness," but it was always shot through with something unbalanced, heedless, undomesticated, fearful.

This is a journey with one of America's wildest families. There is an ebb and flow to *American Bloods*, in this story of a nation, of a family who continually explored life and its extremes. From the outset, the Bloods aimed to secure the necessities of life, which in our history often turned on thieving, occupying, and settling. But mere life was never enough for this growing clan: something like liberty was required, a freedom worth fighting for, expansive like the night sky. As the nineteenth century progressed, driven by machinists and survivors, a certain retrenchment of life and its pursuits took hold in the United States, a mitering and channeling of stargazing liberties. But in the second half of the century, as the nation turned on itself and came undone, minds and souls were once again loosed upon the world, and lovers and spirit-seekers sought to make good on a nation's promise—of being again and always happily free. The Bloods circulated through each era, an animating force of

American history, just below the surface—proving themselves, time and again, larger than life. This is a dynasty of the most literal sort—"a seat of power" that shaped and unsettled a nation as it came into its own.

ON THE BRISK morning of October 30, 1692, John Blood gathered up his rifle and called to his dogs. It was time to clear the swamp of unwanted beasts. He loped into the woods along the bridle trail that once skirted the Concord River. Woods may, as Robert Frost wrote, be "lovely, dark and deep," but the word "woods" has its root in an ancient term for unruliness, or more precisely, madness. John went into the wilds, searching for something, and never came home.

This is the story of John's family, the story of the American Bloods.

Frederic Remington, *Moonlight, Wolf,* 1904

PART I

LIFE

THE THIEF ≣

The lion cannot protect himself from traps, and
the fox cannot defend himself from wolves. One
must therefore be a fox to recognize traps, and a
lion to frighten wolves.

—NICCOLÒ MACHIAVELLI, *THE PRINCE*, 1532[1]

A CENTURY BEFORE THE AMERICAN REVOLUTION,
Blood Farm was set on land owned by the British Crown. The
Crown, however, had no actual hold on the American Bloods.
To the Bloods, the Crown was a symbol to be challenged. And
for one of them, it also was an object to be stolen.

TODAY, 23,578 GEMSTONES are housed under glass, under
armed guard, at the Jewel House in the Tower of London. At
the center of the collection of gems is the Imperial State Crown,
which, for a thousand years, has been worn by British monarchs as they exit Westminster Abbey after their coronation.
If there is a single symbol of monarchical rule, a symbol that
stood against the fledgling colonies of America, this is it. Used

in celebrations throughout the year, it is a sort of everyday crown, the crown of state business. Due to its regular use, the crown has been modified, repaired, and replaced numerous times. Now it features 2,916 jewels, including Cullinan II, or the Second Star of Africa, a cushion-cut diamond with sixty-six facets, weighing 317.4 carats. But Cullinan II, a relatively recent addition to the royal regalia, is not the focal point of the crown. Seated just above this brilliant clear cushion, squarely on the forehead of nobility, rests the oldest, most mysterious gem in the Tower: the Black Prince's Ruby.

In 1919, when George Younghusband studied the Crown Jewels, he remarked that this ruby "has belonged to the royal house since 1367. Its history before that date is unknown and may be of great antiquity, for it is pierced at one end, so as to be worn as a pendant, as often are gems of Oriental origin, and the Orient is exceedingly old."[2] We now know that before 1367, the ruby was owned by the king of Moorish Granada, and coveted by Don Pedro, the king of Castile, who took the most expeditious path to seizing it by stabbing his adversary to death. Pedro, often known as Peter the Cruel, went on to vie for the Spanish throne, allying himself with England. In April 1367, at the bloody Battle of Nájera—with the help of mercenaries funded by the British monarchy—Pedro came to power. The new king of Spain occasionally paid his debts, and, in this case, passed the ruby to the Black Prince, the son of Edward III of England. The stone, now a symbol of violence and theft, became the central decoration of the royal family. When England and France crossed swords at the Battle of Agincourt in 1415, in one of the greatest English victories in the Hundred Years' War, the ruby was there, affixed to the battle helmet of Henry V. According to legend, Henry received a glancing head blow that removed part of the helmet, but the king's head and the Black Prince's Ruby remained attached, and the rock became a symbol of unlikely victory. In the centuries following the victory at Agincourt, the gem was placed squarely on the front cross pattée of the Imperial State Crown, and the crown, along with the royal scepter and orb, was placed with great care into a designated room, first at Westminster Abbey and then at the Tower of London—where it remained almost secure.[3] Almost.

It was stolen exactly once.

Thomas Blood came by his thieving ways as honestly as any man could.

He was cousin to the earliest American Bloods. Their family originally hailed from Northumberland, the northernmost region of England abutting the Scottish border. The Blood

The British Crown Jewels

family was founded, not unlike America itself, in the promise and peril of a nameless border region—a site of trespassing and looting. The New World was envisioned centuries before it was discovered, in a pointed sense of lack, in an abiding discontent with one's origins and home. The insecurity experienced by the earliest American colonists, four hundred years later, was presaged by the medieval mindset of the inhabitants of the wild moors.

Today, Northumberland is a thinly populated territory, a desolate highland more amenable to roe deer than humans. In the thirteenth century, the land of the Bloods was even more barren, and wolves roamed freely, attacking its few inhabitants and digging up its slowly expanding graveyards. The heath had been the site of military conflict for more than a millennium, hard, unforgiving ground better for galloping across and dying on than putting down roots in.[4] The Bloods lived but miles from Hadrian's Wall, erected in AD 123 to defend Roman civilization from the Picts. The wall did nothing to repel the seafaring Vikings who ransacked the region in the eighth century. This was a haunted land, long in flux, where territories simultaneously meet and part ways, a seat of contention and unrest. Loyalties at the border are fluid, or just as often, nonexistent. In such a place, the only constant is the specter of homelessness. By the mid-sixteenth century, the Bloods had temporarily pledged themselves to the British Crown, and fought on its behalf against the Irish magnate Hugh O'Neill, who aimed to sever Ireland from British rule. The Bloods, however, were never Royalists in any formal and lasting sense, only opportunists who understood conflict as a way of carving out a home, even on an island as unforgiving as this one.

Thomas Blood was born at Sarney in County Meath,

twenty miles north of Dublin, in 1618. Very little is known about his childhood save for the fact that he grew up in a world that had come undone. What was once the British kingdom was now torn into three, and the Wars of the Three Kingdoms, the British Civil Wars, were underway, collectively known as the English Civil War. As a boy, Thomas learned quickly that his family lived in singularly chaotic times—times in which thievery did not preclude respectability and social status. His grandfather Edmund lived at Kilnaboy Castle overlooking the North Atlantic and controlled a stretch of water—most likely Liscannor Bay—between Limerick and Galway. A merchant on his way to either town had to pass through Blood's waters, which was, it turned out, an unusually expensive trip: Edmund Blood, supported by a fleet of cutter ships and crews of armed men, suggested that the captain of each vessel surrender part of their load, or comparable moneys, in return for safe passage. This is to say that Thomas Blood was the youngest grandson of a wealthy pirate, a boy who learned early on that criminality was one of the few paths to prosperity.

Thomas came of age in the political landscape of seventeenth-century Britain, demarcated along strict, but circuitous, religious lines. Catholics would fight Protestants, but Protestantism itself would schism and members of various factions would take up arms against their fellow Reformists. Religion was a matter of devotion and piety, but it also determined whom one was licensed to murder and torture.

The crisis might have been avoided, or at least mitigated, had the religious groups been separated geographically. But they weren't. So neighbor was pitted against neighbor across the kingdom in what the English philosopher Thomas Hobbes—who lived through the Civil War—lamented was "a warre of everyone against everyone." "Warre," for Hobbes, connoted a state of anarchy in which bloody conflict, if not faced at every moment, remained a constant and inescapable threat, a state of thoroughgoing apprehension punctuated by merciless violence.[5] This described the Ireland of Thomas Blood's day rather nicely, which explains a lot about the darkly authoritarian vision of Hobbes's *Leviathan*. It is telling, and foreboding, that Thomas, at the tender age of twenty-two, in 1640, was made a justice of the peace. What peace meant, however, was anybody's guess.

Thomas spent his early twenties killing in the name of Charles I: the prospect of getting rich somehow had a way of solidifying commitments that might otherwise have been unstable. And he did get rich, plundering the farms of his enemies and stealing their land. When the Scottish rebellion inspired Irish Catholics to revolt at Ulster in October 1641—and later establish the Catholic Confederation, which became the country's de facto government—Blood was among the Royalists who fought successfully to restore English rule. In the next year, Thomas raised the banner against the Parliamentary forces of Oliver Cromwell, and this "Captain Bludd," now a quartermaster, emerged in the roll call of Royalist troops in Sir Lewis Dyve's regiment of infantry forces. The king's forces, however, were beginning to take heavy losses, and at some point in the mid-1640s, Thomas Blood reevaluated his commitment to Charles I and joined the Parliamentary army. This would be the wisest choice of Thomas's notorious life.

On January 30, 1649, on a bitingly cold afternoon, Charles I was led under armed guard from St. James's Palace, where he had been placed under house arrest, to the Palace of Whitehall. A scaffold had been erected outside the Banqueting House. In the weeks before, he had been tried and convicted of treason.

Charles had argued that liberty and freedom could only be secured by a good and stable monarch, a political order that only he, the rightful king, could secure, but then he followed up with an assertion that Cromwell and his soldiers could not abide: such freedom did not involve subjects being *part* of this government, that "a subject and a sovereign are clean different things."[6] Different indeed. To the very end, Charles Stuart— for that is what the Parliamentarians called him—maintained that he was king and "the king could do no wrong." Sovereign immunity, however, had lost its power. Wrong or right, Charles was going to die. In the king's last words, "I go from a corruptible to an incorruptible Crown, where no disturbance can be, no disturbance in the World."[7] At two o'clock in the afternoon, a masked executioner mounted the scaffold, cut off Charles's head, and ushered him to the only place where there is absolutely no disturbance. A quiet groan supposedly swept through the once-frenzied crowd around Whitehall, like a sigh of relief so total that it escapes as a moan, or a lament that grows into a stifled cry. In the days that followed the execution, Oliver Cromwell visited Charles's reassembled body (his head having been reattached for burial), and it is said that he uttered two Machiavellian words: "Cruel necessity."[8] Woe to the man who tries to deny the danger of unrealistic ambitions. For Royalists, the beheading of Charles I meant something very different; it was tantamount to the death of God, and, as Dostoyevsky would later write, "when God is dead everything is permitted."

Thomas Blood hadn't waited for Charles I to be beheaded before turning on his king. By the early 1650s, he was firmly ensconced in the Parliamentary army as a lieutenant, and when Cromwell was named the lord protector of the Commonwealth in 1653, Blood was among his supporters who would share in the bounty of victory. Blood returned to Ireland, a territory that was being repartitioned by Parliament; lands once owned by Royalists and Catholics were given to Cromwell's allies. By 1652, Blood owned approximately 2,500 very profitable acres in the counties surrounding Dublin and Sarney. He also had a son, Thomas, born to a very respectable wife, Maria Holcrofte, daughter of Thomas Holcrofte, the mayor of Liverpool. During these years of good fortune, Blood was in direct service to Cromwell, who considered him "a person fit for employment and promotion."[9] What Blood's exact employment consisted of is largely a matter of speculation but he undoubtedly supported his lord protector in initiating the largest campaign of ethnic cleansing of the British Isles since the Norman conquest, which displaced or killed more than fifty thousand Irish Catholics. Good fortune came at a wolfish price.

For most of the 1650s, Thomas Blood's family lived on in the good graces of their new leader. "Cruel necessity," however, does not pick sides, and in 1658, Cromwell, who was by that time regarded as "Prince Oliver," died. Any pretenses to strict Protestantism—like the Puritanism that had been suppressed under the Royalists—died with him. John Evelyn reported in his diary of November 22, 1658, that he witnessed "the superb funeral of the Protector . . . but it was the joyfullest funeral that [he] ever saw, for there were none that cried, but dogs, which the souldiers hooted away with a barbarous noise; drinking and taking tobacco in the streets as they went."[10] In the absence of a fear-inducing, often self-righteous ruler, civil society again risked tipping into chaos, and the Protectorate of England was fully dissolved in May 1659.

The English Crown—which had remained in exile in France for many years—would return to London victorious just two years after the death of Cromwell. Actually, the crowns and the rest of the royal jewels had to be replaced or recovered since most of them had been melted down and sold off after the execution of Charles I. His successor spared no expense in this project and many of his subjects hoped that the monarchy could once again be secured.

Thomas Blood, however, was not enthused.

The restoration of the monarchy in 1660, with the coronation of Charles II, ushered in a series of events that made his life nearly unbearable. The Irish Parliament passed the Act of Settlement, which forced Cromwellian soldiers like Blood to forfeit much of the acreage they had been granted in the land grab in Ireland. Blood lost more than three-quarters of his estate. It was this turn of events that transformed him into both a criminal and a legend that followed the American Bloods to a New World.

DUBLIN, 1661. The cattle of a butcher named Dolan vanished. Wolves still roamed the Irish countryside, but, in this instance, they weren't responsible. On June 30, Dolan visited James Butler, the first Duke of Ormond, to file a legal grievance in order to retrieve his "outlandish bull and cow." The thief was none other than "a lieutenant in the late army," Thomas Blood. The cattle were returned, and the Bloods presumably went hungry. This minor offense reflects the direness of Blood's financial situation, of a man who could hardly live hand to mouth, but also sets the stage for his growing hatred for the Duke of Ormond, and more generally, for the Crown.

To call Ormond a Royalist would be a gross understatement. When Charles II fled England during Cromwell's reign,

Ormond accompanied his king to France. When Charles II reclaimed the throne in 1660, Ormond was rewarded, being named lord high steward, the first of the Great Offices of State, the right hand of the king. In November 1661, he assumed the lord lieutenancy of Ireland, took up residency at Dublin Castle, and crossed paths and swords with Thomas Blood.[11] Blood, at that moment, was after more than cattle—he wanted nothing less than a castle, Dublin Castle—and he began to conspire with other former Parliamentarians to recapture it. He was on the fringes of a small, unsuccessful plot to overturn the government, but he quickly moved into a principal role in a much wider, more deadly conspiracy against Ormond.

In the winter of 1662, Blood journeyed north into the heart of the Gaelic world—the northern province of Ulster, a historically wild realm that Irish and Scots had co-occupied for centuries. Here Blood found allies: Presbyterian Scots who had recently settled in the region, who promised to support his plan to seize the castle and usurp the Irish government headed by Ormond. According to Royalist spymasters, Blood's insurrection was part of a wider plan to overthrow Charles II, coordinated with radical Protestant uprisings in England and Ireland. The rumblings of revolution—or civil war—began to sound once again. The duke wrote to Charles II that "the general discontent will not, I hope cause any disturbance but if it should, the army is in a very ill state to repress it . . . If we cannot keep the army together it will always be in the power of a few desperate men to start a commotion with regard to which no one can say where it will end."[12]

On the evening of May 20, 1663, Blood and a few desperate men—seven to be precise—met at the White Hart in Dublin, a thatched, whitewashed pub in the shadow of the early Gothic

St. Patrick's Cathedral. The coup was to be as simple as it was dangerous: in the morning, three of the men were to dress as petitioners, like the butcher Dolan, and seek Ormond's assistance in legal grievances. When the trio was granted access to the Great Gate, a fourth man, disguised as a baker, would create a diversion and the guards would be subdued or killed. This is where Blood would come in: leading a hundred soldiers, he'd storm the castle and capture Ormond. They would raise the flag of the insurgency and Protestant troops would march under the banner, freeing Ireland from popery and royal control.[13]

Unfortunately for Blood, none of that happened. Among the desperate men at the White Hart was Phillip Alden, who double-crossed Blood. Just hours after the conspirators left the pub, Alden contacted his handler, the spymaster Ned Vernon. Before dawn, Ormond was roused and given news of the plot, and quarters of Dublin woke, almost immediately, to the sound of his soldiers battering in doors and seizing the conspirators.

Part of Blood's band entered Dublin Castle—but not as they had intended. A handful entered in manacles, under armed guard. Blood was not among the captured. Three days later, Ormond offered one hundred pounds for the arrest of thirteen organizers of this "traitorous plot." The first name on the list of escapees was Thomas Blood. Had he been captured, he certainly would have faced a gruesome end of torture and death, but Blood fled to the mountainous region north of Dublin, then to Scotland, and finally to the Dutch Low Countries. Several of the schemers were not nearly as lucky—they were hung at Ormond's orders. Explaining his handling of the coup, Ormond wrote to Charles II: "We [must] show that we are prepared to foil such attempt" but also show "they mean absolute ruin to the contrivers."[14] Blood, however, lived on. The seizure of Dublin Castle had failed, but it succeeded in one important respect: it gave Thomas Blood the opportunity to express the high-minded motivation for his dissent, an intention that would be carried forth on American soil by the Bloods who crossed the Atlantic. Taking up arms was the proper response to one's personhood or estate being unjustly taken. Before attacking Ormond's stronghold, Blood had written out the public objectives of the rebellion:

> Having long expected the securing of our lives, liberties and estates as a reasonable recompense for that industry and diligence exercised by the Protestants of this kingdom . . . instead we find ourselves, our wives and children, without mercy, delivered as a prey unto these barbarous and bloody murderers, whose inhumane cruelty is . . . in the blood of 150,000 poor Protestants . . . And to this end . . . no well-minded Protestants in the three kingdoms may be afraid to stand by us in this our just quarrel, we will stand for liberty of conscience proper to everyone as a Christian for establishing the Protestant religion in purity, according to the Solemn League and Covenant.[15]

This religiously inflected declaration carried with it a practical demand for "restoring each person to his lands as they held them in the year 1659," the year that Blood was dispossessed of his estate. Blood's statement, however, was justification not only for his particular form of rebellion but also for a broader revolution based on a political philosophy that was beginning to show itself in the 1660s. Written in 1663, Blood's protection of the "lives, liberties and estates" of the people drew directly on the language used in the Declaration of Breda, the 1660 writ of

Charles II that ensured that no harm would come to Parliamentarians for their actions against the king during the Civil War or the Interregnum. At Breda, Charles II had stated that "no crime committed either against him or his royal father shall (as far as lies in his Majesty's power) endamage the least either in lives, liberties, estates, or reputation; it being his Majesty's desire that all sorts of discord should be laid aside among all his subjects."[16] Blood, a commoner, was now using the king's words against him. Life, liberty, land, and riches could not be stripped from a person without consequences. A hundred years later, this thought would take hold in the New World as inalienable rights, an ideal that supported the American Bloods in their own bloody revolt against the Crown.

AFTER THE FAILED PLOT against Ormond, Thomas Blood went into hiding. He was described as a "stout fellow," a stocky man in his late forties, with a pockmarked face, deep-set eyes, meaty jowls, and a fleshy, imposing nose. He was considered an unattractive man, suited for unattractive jobs. He was reputedly the champion—or henchman—of the Earl of Buckingham and would often face Buckingham's opponents when things got dirty. The clearest portrait of him was produced by Gilbert (or Gerard) Soest, who also painted Shakespeare and Samuel Butler.[17] The title of the portrait, however, is peculiar: *Unknown Man, Formerly Known as Thomas Blood.*[18] During these years Blood was known as Dr. Ayliffe or Dr. Allen in Romford Market, east of London, pretending to practice as a physician and apothecary.

This was not a happy time for Blood, and he laid most of the blame for his sorrows at the feet of his longtime nemesis,

Gilbert Soest,
Unknown Man,
Formerly Known
as Thomas Blood

the Duke of Ormond. By 1670, Ormond had returned to London and taken up residence at Clarendon House, which was, in the words of John Evelyn, "the best contriv'd, the most useful, graceful and magnificent house in England."[19] When Ormond traveled, he would usually leave his quarters by coach and head north on St. James's Street, accompanied by only a small handful of footmen. Thomas Blood was silently taking note. On the night of December 6, 1670, Blood and three armed accomplices attacked Ormond's coach, dragged the duke into the street, bound him, affixed a notice of offenses to his chest, and spurred him on to the northeast corner of Hyde Park. They were on their way to Tyburn, or more specifically the Tyburn Tree: London's most famous gallows. The triangular structure could accommodate twenty-four men, or corpses, at a time and public hangings occurred twelve times a year. The poet John Taylor wrote of Tyburn: "I have heard sundry men oft times dispute/ Of trees, that in one year will twice bear fruit./ But if a man note Tyburn, 'will appear,/ That that's a tree that bears twelve times a year.'"[20] Ormond was to have the tree all to himself. Capital punishment was meted out at other places, too—the Tower of London was for traitors, West Smithfield for witches— but Tyburn was specifically for felons. And this is what Ormond was in Blood's eyes: the basest of thieves. By horse, at night, the trip from Piccadilly to Tyburn could be made in a matter of minutes, but Ormond freed himself en route and escaped back into the narrow, winding streets of Mayfair, which have the uncanny ability to make things and people suddenly vanish.

In the seventeenth century, there were two kinds of thieves: the type, like Ormond, who expanded their already generous holdings by stealing from the common people, and the type, like the famous highwaymen of the day, who got rich by steal- ing from nobility. A highwayman's luck eventually ran out and he would be run to Tyburn, but rogues like Ormond rarely met this fate, instead hiding in their ill-gotten mansions, on the es- tates that had once belonged to men like Blood. For the time being, Blood would continue to suffer this inequity without compensation.

"MONUMENTS OF SUPERSTITION and idolatry." These were Oliver Cromwell's words in describing the Crown Jewels, which were "symbolic of the detestable rule of kings."[21] When this detestable rule returned with Charles II, so too did the gems. In previous ages, these monuments to absolute power were far removed from the common people, but Charles II decided that it was probably best to make the crown slightly more accessible, placing the jewels in a viewing room in the Tower of London.

For a small fee, a single guard would allow visitors to inspect the glittering royal objects. The protection was casual given the immensity of their value. Cattle, castle, and now a duke: Thomas Blood was a failed thief and a would-be murderer. The pious Protestant radicals who had long befriended Blood began to turn on him. There was only one way for him to redeem himself. After another failed assassination attempt on Ormond, Blood immediately turned his attention to the jewels.

The Master of the Jewel House, the aged Talbot Edwards, lived with his wife and daughter in a small apartment in the Tower of London. He was not a wealthy man, but pious and as generous as his circumstances would allow. Blood considered him an easy mark. The plan involved multiple deceptions: Blood would dress as an Anglican parson (this was no small matter for a Presbyterian); he would accompany his "wife," a close female friend, to the Tower on the pretense of a typical visit to marvel over the jewels; his "wife" would feign sickness and be taken to Edwards's apartment; the good parson would thank the old couple profusely over the coming weeks; in time, Blood would suggest that his wealthy "nephew" marry the Edwardses' daughter; eventually a dinner with several guests would be held at the Tower to initiate the courtship.[22] The plan went off without a hitch.

The dinner was arranged for the evening of May 9; Blood, the "nephew," and two friends were invited. The two friends arrived at the Tower carrying canes. At Blood's request, Edwards took the party to the Jewel House, unlocking the grate that protected the crown, scepter, and royal orb, and was immediately accosted by the men, who turned out to be heavily armed: Blood carried dungeon daggers and a pistol, and the canes of his companions concealed rapiers.[23] One of the assailants later admitted that they "clapped a gag in Edwards' mouth which was a great plug of wood with a small hole in the middle to take breath" and tied him up "in waxed leathers . . . and they fastened an iron hook to his nose that no sound might pass from him."[24] Edwards was bludgeoned to the brink of death with what in the medieval world was called a "beetle," an oversized mallet that was usually used for pounding paving stones in place. A word about dungeon daggers: these are knives designed for exactly one purpose. Slender and nearly a foot in length, they are meant to be concealed, drawn, and used to impale a human body, like that of the hapless Tower guard. Complications from the wounds sustained in this knife attack would, years later, lead to the old man's premature death.

With the guard tied and subdued, the thieves could work in peace. Swiftly. The Imperial State Crown was light and valuable—the ruby of the Black Prince is essentially priceless—but a crown is unwieldy and slightly conspicuous in its traditional wearable form. So, in what seemed like a reasonable decision, Blood used the beetle to break the crown down to more manageable, concealable proportions. The thief dislodged the jewel and pocketed it. A similar mode of disassembly was attempted on the royal scepter, but the scepter proved much harder to partition. A file was employed and the staff of power eventually came apart. The orb proved to be the real problem until a third man shoved it down his pants. Then the men ran, as best they could with the haul, for their horses that stood waiting at the gate. Time was running out. Help was on its way; the guard rallied to his feet, shouting, "Treason! Murder! The crown is stolen!" The chase was on. The thieves fled, making for the Iron Gate on the banks of the Thames. They would have made it had it not been for Edwards's son Wythe, a former soldier recently returned from the Flanders campaign, who witnessed the escape and sounded the alarm. Blood supposedly fought his captives to the very end, crying, "It was a gallant attempt, however unsuccessful! It was for a crown!"[25] In the shadow of the ivy-laden Iron Gate tower, guardsmen finally captured the leader of the heist, a man who instantly became the most notorious thief in England. Thomas Blood was thrown in chains and imprisoned in the Tower of London.

THE TOWER OF LONDON is a site of ambivalence. Its central keep, the White Tower, was constructed by William the Conqueror in 1066, as an indomitable sign of his conquest and occupation of London. But by the thirteenth century, it would become the place where Richard II was imprisoned and ultimately abdicated the throne. The Tower was meant to stand for royal loyalty, but Blood knew that it could also provide shelter for a turncoat; it was a place where lives were lost but also won. Blood informed his guards, and then his interrogators, that he would speak to no one but the king himself.

Charles II was known as the "Merry Monarch," and he supposedly laughed and acquiesced when he heard Blood's demand. The bald audacity of the crime and the rogue's lack of remorse struck the king as good a reason as any to grant

Blood an audience. Even prior to Blood coming before the king on May 11, it was almost certain that Blood would be spared. Ormond, in some dismay, explained to his friend the diplomat-landowner Robert Southwell that "no king would see a malefactor" but only with "the intention of a pardon."[26] But first, Blood had to make his argument. Before the king, he immediately admitted that he'd attacked Ormond out of sworn revenge, and, similarly, had tried to steal the Crown Jewels as recompense for injuries to his person and estate, "for disgraces and disappointments he had met in Ireland."[27]

At the end of her life, at the beginning of the seventeenth century, Elizabeth I had lamented the state of her island kingdom, declaring that she had sent "wolves, not shepherds, to govern Ireland, for they have left me nothing to govern over but ashes and carcasses."[28] Two generations later, Charles II understood that wolves such as Thomas Blood were still on the prowl, and had to be appeased. At the end of the audience with Charles II, the monarch asked the prisoner: "What if I give you your life?" Blood responded with characteristic boldness: "I should endeavor to deserve it."[29]

Instead of taking his head, the king gave Blood a handsome pension and a place in the royal court. How this happened is not entirely clear. But certain likelihoods point in three possible directions. The king could have rightly identified Blood as a man who could be of use, a shadowy character who was willing to act in self-interest rather than any enduring loyalty. He may have also been encouraged by the Duke of Buckingham, Blood's enduring friend and patron, to spare the thief's life. Or it could have been Charles II, forever financially pinched, who hired Blood to steal his *own* Crown Jewels—a ploy that could have filled his coffers if only for a little while. What supports this last theory is a letter written by Blood to the king, dated May 19, 1671. Blood accused a treasurer of the navy of paying him to venture the crime; "know your friends," the thief advised the king. In the years that followed, it often seemed that Blood himself was the king's closest companion.[30]

The real reason for Charles II's unlikely pardon of Blood may never be known, but one thing is certain: Blood was free to leave the Tower and undoubtedly did so with more money and a better reputation than he had enjoyed since the Restoration. He came to reside on Bowling Alley, now Bowling Street, a convenient distance from Whitehall, where he was often called to advise the king. In 1672, as England was embroiled in the Franco-Dutch War, it was Thomas Blood who intercepted military correspondence from Holland, and it was Thomas Blood who gauged political dissent on the home front. It now appeared that he worked at the service of the Crown, and in the final years of his life he may have come to deserve the pardon that Charles II had granted.[31]

Blood's return to the good graces of the king may not have surprised members of the royal court, but news of the man's robbery, pardon, and subsequent employment by Charles II circulated through London for decades. The rakish second Earl of Rochester, John Wilmot, before dying of venereal disease, quipped:

> *Blood, that wears treason in his face,*
> *Villain complete in parson's gown,*
> *How much he is at court in grace*
> *For stealing Ormond and the crown!*

Since loyalty does no man good,
Let's steal the King, and outdo Blood![32]

In fact, no one ever outdid Blood: after the theft, the jewels were returned to the Tower and placed under armed guard, where they remain to this day. The ornaments of sovereignty were secure, but the escapades of Thomas Blood underscored the deep instability of the English monarchy. That a man like Blood could come so close to stealing the Crown, that he was pardoned and then employed by this selfsame government, that he could then take up residence just steps from Buckingham Palace—these were signs of a government's fragility and vulnerability. There was no grand strategy or realpolitik, just the tactics of individuals, in ever-changing coalition, scrapping for any semblance of power. Life has a certain mercenary quality, one driven, in no small part, by the fact that authorities can neither sufficiently terrify nor adequately secure their subjects. In such an environment, political wolves like Blood flourished.

Blood died on August 24, 1680, and was buried in St. Margaret's Church in Westminster. On his grave, now long destroyed, was written the epitaph: "Here lies the man who boldly hath run through More villainies than England ever knew; And ne'er to any friend he had was true. Here let him then by all unpitied lie, And let's rejoice his time was come to die."[33] Many, however, believed that this too was an act of trickery—that Blood had staged his own demise in order to escape a fine and court proceedings. To lay these suspicions to rest once and for all, in the days that followed Blood's burial, the body was disinterred and the identity of the corpse supposedly confirmed thanks to Blood's abnormally large thumb that had often been used to identify him, twice the size of a normal digit. Today, some people call this abnormality "royal." Others call it a "murderer's thumb."[34] The rumors continued to swirl: Thomas Blood had escaped to the New World, a place more suited to his savagery. It was, after all, the frontier home of his closest kin, the American Bloods.

THE SETTLERS

> If the Indians were as other people are and did manage their war fairly after the manner of other nations it might be looked upon as inhuman to pursue them in such a manner. But they are to be looked upon as thieves and murderers and do acts without proclaiming war, they do not appear openly in the field to bid us battle . . . they act like wolves and are to be dealt withal as wolves.
>
> —REV. JOHN STOPPARD TO
> GOVERNOR DUDLEY OF MASSACHUSETTS, 1703[1]

IN THE MINDS OF THE NEW ENGLAND COLONISTS, there was a strict division between civilization and wilderness, a distinction between honorable soldiers and ruthless murderers, a meaningful difference between the hunter and the hunted. Indeed, living on the border seemed to necessitate and instantiate this sort of Manichean vision of the world. The first Blood brothers of New England—Robert, John, and James—were frontiersmen and understood this polarity, but they were also the nephews of Thomas Blood the jewel thief, and acknowledged the violent contradictions that came to define the seventeenth century. They understood that even civilized men could act like wolves, and rogues could come close to seizing the crown. The brothers were thousands of miles away when their uncle would test this point in England, but circumstances in the New World would teach them a lesson that Thomas knew well—that human existence was not cleanly demarcated but unshakably wild. One of the first American Bloods came to live in the no-man's-land to the north of Concord surrounding Wolf Rock, seated just above Tophet Swamp, on the edge of a new nation. The lesson would be learned by heart.

Robert Blood was born in 1628, in Ruddington on the outskirts of Nottingham, the stronghold of the English Bloods.[2] He was the youngest of at least three Blood men who, to a greater or lesser extent, traveled together across the Atlantic, arriving on the shores of Massachusetts during the Great Migration of the 1630s. The Bloods arrived as part of one of the first waves of Puritans who came to inhabit Colonial America, driven abroad by Charles I's repression and persecution of religious sects. Given their later contact with the governor, John Winthrop, they may have been members of the Winthrop Fleet that arrived in Salem in April 1630.[3] Or they would have arrived shortly thereafter. Some Bloods, like Thomas Blood, sought temporary safety in Ireland, but others had to take more extreme forms of flight to escape the violence of Charles I. The question remained: Could they find a way to live apart from the Crown?

In coming to America, the Puritans had chosen self-imposed exile; this ensured their religious freedom but also jeopardized their claims to a cultural heritage. They risked losing, in Jill Lepore's word, their "Englishness."[4] To counteract this danger—to guard against slipping into savagery—it was necessary to maintain both their "pure" Protestantism and the trappings of European society (its ways of conversing, eating, entertaining, and trading). This was going to be difficult since the worldliness of seventeenth-century Great Britain, epitomized by the Star Chamber Court of Charles I, was regarded by Puritans as completely out of sync with Christian piety. The trick, it seemed, was to reframe society around a new set of virtues.

That is what John Winthrop attempted to do in a sermon titled "A Model of Christian Charity," written on the ship *Arbella* en route to Massachusetts in 1630.[5] The new colony—as opposed to the corruption that had claimed Europe—was to be based on two principles: justice and mercy. It was to be an exceptional place that stood not only as a political exemplar but, more importantly, as a moral one. "The Lord will be our God, and delight to dwell among us, as His own people," Winthrop proclaimed. "He shall make us a praise and glory that men shall say of succeeding plantations, 'may the Lord make it like that of New England.' For we must consider that we shall be as a city upon a hill. The eyes of all people are upon us."[6] It was a nice thought. Justice and mercy, for Winthrop, were the only palliatives for the moral and religious degradation the Puritans had narrowly escaped. England, like the rest of Europe, was a lost cause, lost to two almost unstoppable forces: the godless self-interest of noblemen like Ormond, and the hubristic pretenses of monarchs who thought they were God. What was needed was a *New* England, based on Scripture, in which citizens prioritized public interests—the commonweal—over selfish desires. If settlers like the Bloods were to acquire land, it was, at least in theory, going to be with the permission of Winthrop, who would insist on the preservation of these ideals.

Upon arriving in New England, it was James rather than Robert who was the first Blood to mark the historical record, setting up his home in Concord prior to 1639. Before the town was established in 1636, it had a more general name: Musketaquid, the Algonquin word meaning "grassy plain." This low-lying area at the confluence of two great rivers had been occupied by Native peoples for more than three thousand years. The rivers—which today have morphed into the shallow and lazy Assabet and the Sudbury—at the time eddied in deep holes and teemed with fish. The Pennacook Indians established weirs in the rivers' pools and planted corn along their banks. It was, at least before the Europeans arrived, a place of concord—utter peace. In 1616, however, a smallpox plague (brought by white explorers) swept the Musketaquid and decimated the population.[7] When settlers like Blood, led by Simon Willard, entered the region in 1636, the Native people regarded them as harbingers of death. It is in this context that a peaceful land agreement was struck with the sagamore leaders and tranquil Concord was founded. James Blood's house was at the absolute center of it—the site for a hulking gray clapboard colonial, which today is known as the Old Manse.

James Blood's home would become one of the most iconic in the history of American letters. It was rented to Nathaniel Hawthorne in 1842 as a writer's retreat; before that, in 1836, Ralph Waldo Emerson drafted his seminal essay "Nature" in the manse's upstairs study. The Old Manse was owned by William Ralph Emerson, the transcendentalist's grandfather, the chaplain of the Continental Army; even at the time, it overlooked Old North Bridge, the birthplace of the Revolution. Two hundred years before this "shot heard round the world," however, the inner keeping rooms of the Old Manse formed the cozy center of James Blood's home. In 1640, Winthrop granted Blood more than five hundred acres of arable land that stretched north from the current site of the manse. Blood planted an orchard and took up farming, growing enough corn, rye, cabbages, and turnips to last his family through the bitter New England winters.

For a Blood, James was a very respectable man. On June 2, 1641, he became a "freeman" in the colony.[8] Today the early American colonies are regarded as safe havens of freedom (for the white settlers in any case), but in the days of the Puritans, they were anything but. Outsiders, including newcomers like James, were regarded with suspicion and their movements were monitored closely in the new settlements of New England. The scrutiny ended only when this sort of common man took the oath of a freeman, of being properly religious, in the traditional sense of the word. The Congregational ministers of the colonies were the gatekeepers of freedom, which entitled a man to the civil and political rights of a free government. Core governmental commitments that the Puritans loathed in an English context were ferociously revived in Colonial America: liberty depended on obedience and loyalty. This was the core of the formal oath that James Blood took. And this was the tacit agreement that he embraced in making a home on the banks of the Concord River. James's brethren, however, would only partially keep it.

ROBERT, ASSOCIATED WITH but distant from James, was a freeman, but of a very different sort: a scoundrel who has been described as "untamed, independent, even unruly."[9] Freedom to him was not secured by yoking oneself to the strictures of society but by breaking free. In relation to James, Robert appears as a sort of prodigal son—or a disobedient younger brother—always on the outskirts of James's sphere of influence and reputation. He was happy enough to benefit from James's standing in the Concord community or the General Assembly when it was expedient, but never for too long or in a way that would place him in lasting debt. As a teenager, Robert parted ways with James, taking up residence in the seaside town of Lynn, which is nestled on Massachusetts Bay between Boston and Salem. But he couldn't stay there long. When contemporary historians investigate references to "violent speech" in the New World, they typically observe the relative paucity of written remarks, but then many of them observe that discussions about Robert Blood and his brother are a notable exception. The Lynn presentments of September 5, 1647, report that "Robert Blood [was] presented for abusing William Knight in provoking speeches, challenging him to a fight, pushing him with his arm and breaking his fence in which he had impounded some of his cattle; and for abusing Henry Rodes, seeking to take away a tree that belonged to Rodes, pushing him with his arm and threatening him."[10] Taking away a tree? The court documents suggest that Robert was joined by his brother John, who shared his adversarial approach to civil society: "John Blood [has been] presented for uttering mutinous words in a public place, tending to disturbance of the peace."[11] The Bloods were notorious hell-raisers. By the end of 1647, Robert and John decided, or were asked, or were forced, to leave—and it appears that they set off directly for the home of James Blood. They were to live, in the words of their contemporaries, "neer Concord" but never inside.[12]

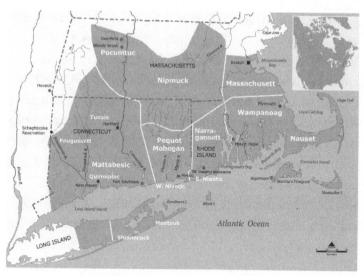

Native American communities of New England circa 1680

The Concord community needed men: in 1644 its pastor John Jones had relocated to the Connecticut River Valley and taken nearly an eighth of the town with him, leaving a mere seventy members in the congregation at Concord. Inland settlements only survived by staying large enough to thwart attack. In the following year, the Massachusetts Bay Company made a prohibition against exodus: "In regard of the great danger at Concord . . . will be exposed unto, being inland townes & but thinly peopled, it is ordered that no man inhabiting & settled in any said towns . . . shall remove to any other towne without the allowance of a magistrate . . . until it shall please God to settle peace againe, or some other way of safety to the said townes . . . shall set the inhabitants of the said townes at their former liberty."[13] While European leaders and thinkers were at war over the divinity of the king and the rightful seat of power, the American colonists had narrower, more immediate concerns, namely preserving the integrity of a basic social contract. The social contract is often construed as an agreement between people to live in peaceful and harmonious ways—a contract to be social—but this isn't quite right. Instead, the social contract is an agreement between an individual and his or her government, whereby an individual gives up certain liberties in order to acquire certain goods from the state, goods that he or she could not maintain without the help of an organized authority. The decree concerning Concord's dwindling population echoed an age-old tenet of political philosophy: as Socrates explains in the *Crito*, it would be unjust for a man to abandon his community if he has in the past been raised in, and benefited by, its organization; the first among liberties to place in check was a man's right to opt out of his social obligations. That is, however, exactly what Robert did.

INSTEAD OF MOVING into Concord in 1647, Robert Blood dedicated the next five years to establishing Blood Farm, a three-thousand-acre tract of pasture and woodland, a diamond-shaped plot that stretched from Concord's northern border west to Concord Village (present-day Acton), and north to Billerica. The whole was around four square miles. It was relatively arable land and speculators from Boston and nearby Medford coveted the plot, which was bisected by rivers that fed marshes and graceful pastures, leading to a series of hilltops and high plains. Securing this expanse, however, was no simple project: it involved building stone walls through thick underbrush, surveying impassable swamps, and clearing and maintaining the Native American trails that had once coursed beneath the oak and elm.

Blood lived, quite willingly, on the sharp edge of the state of nature. All the while, he was on the lookout—ever present was the threat of wolves, but still more menacing was the possibility of encountering Indigenous inhabitants who were dissatisfied with the terms of the Concord land agreement. His precarious position was highlighted by a request made to the Massachusetts General Court by the sachem Tahattawan in 1651. The sachem realized that his people were no longer welcome in Concord and therefore requested the "nashope" lands, the supposedly haunted ground of the "roaring hills," close by. The tribe was granted a five-hundred-acre reservation that included Nashoba Hill, a promontory that directly overlooked Tophet Swamp and what became Blood Farm. With the exception of Groton to the north, the Blood land was the most isolated frontier of the new colony.[14]

Like any good thief—or Machiavellian—Robert Blood's success relied on a mixture of temerity and unbelievably good fortune. For Blood, Fortuna wore the visage of Elizabeth Willard, the beautiful daughter of Maj. Simon Willard, one of the original founders of Concord, the commander of the Middlesex militia, and a man who served for forty consecutive years as assistant to the governor and a representative to the General Court. If one needed to grease the wheels of power, Willard was the one to tap. Elizabeth could have chosen from many suitors; indeed, given her independent wealth, she would not have felt the customary draw of matrimony, but somehow she fell in love with this "unruly" American Blood. The couple was married in Concord—as there was no sanctioned church on Blood's plantation—on April 8, 1653.[15] Today, at the Carlisle Historical Society's Heald House Museum, one can still see a fragment of the elaborate frock Elizabeth wore that afternoon:

a silk brocade, almost opulent, as close to royal as any religiously minded colonist would dare.[16]

This was an unusual union. Eligible bachelors came from
legitimate towns. Legitimate towns were, by definition, godly
ones, possessing a Congregational church. Eligible bachelors
were therefore men of God. Robert wasn't. Elizabeth Willard,
on the other hand, was a most eligible bride. What might have
alarmed Elizabeth's Concord neighbors were the terms of the
marriage: Willard's dowry consisted of another thousand acres
that Blood would add to his holdings. Simon Willard instructed
Blood that these lands were not to be sold for profit, but rather
were "for their children and heirs by my daughter." But Robert had no intention of selling. Immediately after the wedding,
Blood successfully confirmed the Native deeds that had been
secured by Elizabeth's father dated June 20, 1642.[17] Marriage
often had the consequence of taming a person's ambitions, but
it is clear that Blood's relationship with Willard had the opposite effect. He had just been given the space and freedom that
men of his family had always craved, and now he was in the
process of creating his estate—existing just beyond the bounds
of Concord—a place where his family could grow unencum-
bered, at the far reaches of society where governments could
not meddle in his affairs. In 1651, the year that Blood turned his
attention to matrimony, the English political theorist Thomas
Hobbes published *De Cive*, writing, "A great family is a kingdom
and a little kingdom a family."[18] Somewhere in between were
the Bloods. Nearly a dozen Blood houses were raised in quick
succession in the vicinity of today's Carlisle, but at the time, according to Robert Blood, on land that belonged to no town or
principality. The Bloods remained what residents of Concord
called "borderers" and "outdwellers," terms that masked the

considerable challenge they posed to the central ideals of the
colonies.

ROBERT BLOOD DID NOT believe in the power of the British
monarchy—or the centralized colonial authority in Boston, for
that matter—but he did understand the rational appeal of the
Hobbesian notion of the social contract, which was meant to
curtail the violence of the English Civil War but was equally
applicable to the need to avoid potential chaos in the American
colonial project. Like Machiavelli, Hobbes "put for the general
inclination of all mankind, a perpetual restless desire of power
after power, that ceaseth only in death."[19] Hobbes, and contract
theorists after him, however, departed from Machiavelli in important ways. Writing in the 1660s, Hobbes held that lasting
cooperation was necessary in order to defend against external
threats and the danger of civil war. Humans were rational, self-
interested agents, but this did not lead them to participate in the
free-for-all described in *The Prince*. Rather, their self-interest—
their desire to avoid misery and maximize gain—encouraged
reasonable men and women to consent to a relatively stable
authority in the hopes of a relatively stable future. The issue for
Blood would have been the scope of the social contract, the assessment of threat, and his family's ability to defend itself. There
were, after all, two types of contract in Hobbes's *Leviathan*: the
type that formed the family, and the kind that laid the basis of
the modern state. Hobbes writes in his little-known "Dialogue
Between a Philosopher and a Student," published as Blood expanded the farm in 1666, that "it is evident that dominion,
government and laws, are far more ancient than history or any
other writing, and that the beginning of all dominion amongst

men was in families."[20] This was an insight that Robert Blood embodied in his private settlement: at certain moments in history, the unity of the family was enough to keep life together.

By the second half of the seventeenth century, Robert and John had both expanded their acreage but also invited relatives to join them on their estates. Robert began to sire a brood of children who would come to protect the increasing number of fields and farms that sprang up in the territory. John, who lived directly adjacent to the Tophet Swamp, by contrast, never married or had children. Instead, he kept a pack of dogs, the type that were good at chasing down invaders. In April 1663 alone, the constable at Billerica paid John for killing two wolves.[21]

It should be said that John was even more of a renegade than his brother Robert. Men living in the colony who were not freemen could take what was called an "oath of fidelity," which granted them the right to vote on community affairs. Everyone, or almost everyone, took this oath, which was administered in the 1640s by none other than Robert's father-in-law, Simon Willard. Robert took the oath. John was the only one in the entire settlement who refused. Blood Farm had its own de facto standing army, bound by blood; in times of relative peace, the Bloods didn't need the protection of Concord to the south or Billerica to the north. They had John Blood. This family, for the time being, held primacy over the state. Indeed, in the 1650s, the Bloods' confidence and ambition knew few bounds. When Groton, the remotest English outpost in New England, was incorporated, two familiar names appeared on the petition: Robert and John Blood.[22] Simon Willard would subsequently move to Groton in 1672, taking up the post of major of the town's frontier militia. Willard's home stood at the single crossroads in the town, the intersection of Main Street and the only road out of town that wound past Gibbet Hill with its rolling pastures dotted with cows, through Blood Farm, then on to Concord and eventually Boston. His house was also the rendezvous point for military explorers westward. Robert Blood was often one of them.

The early 1670s were a period of bounty for the American Bloods, but these years coincided with what many New England thinkers and theologians regarded as a period of ethical and spiritual decline. Winthrop's exalted vision of a "city on a hill," in which the call to commonwealth was to preempt the drive for individual wealth, had all but faded in the decades since the colonists had gained a foothold on the coast. "It was a very sad thing," Winthrop wrote, "how little of a public spirit appeared in the country, but of self-love too much."[23] By the beginning of 1673, the Reverend Increase Mather, father of Cotton Mather and the most prominent minister in Boston at the time, delivered an ominous sermon warning that times of great prosperity are usually times of great decadence and moral degradation. "Great Security is a sign that trouble is near . . . You are asleep in your sins . . . but there's that at hand that will awaken you; you think it is not midnight, but that you may sleep on securely still, but it's morning. So you are asleep, and you think that Judgement is slumbering too, when—as it's waiting ready to take hold on you."[24] Mather's moralizing and handwringing—he was inclined to both—revealed a real problem in the colonies, but it didn't necessarily or exclusively have to do with the spiritual fabric of society. It was also a political crisis. Church membership was down, which was both a sign and a cause of a more significant issue: families like the Bloods were beginning to successfully strike out on their own without the protection (or guidance) of Puritan leaders like Mather.

Towns—the bastions of religion and civilization—were beginning to lose the magnetism they had held over colonial life.
This spelled Mather's "trouble": an ambiguous, dangerous
moment when a people could go astray. As America's frontier
spirit surged, New Englanders like Robert Blood journeyed
deeper into the wilds and, Mather feared, risked losing themselves and jeopardizing the colonies.

This sense of adventure was severely curtailed in 1675 when
King Philip's War erupted. King Philip was not king in the
traditional sense of the word. He was Metacomet, the youngest son of Massasoit, the chief of the Wampanoag Confederacy
who had brokered peace with the members of the Plymouth
Colony in the 1620s. Fifty years later, however, it became clear
to Metacomet that what the colonists meant by "peace" was the
wholesale disarmament and subjugation of the tribes of Massachusetts. In the winter of 1671, Natives were seen sharpening
tomahawks and repairing muskets, and hostilities were averted
only by an agreement made at Taunton in March of that year
for the Wampanoag warriors to turn over their weapons.[25]
Some did, but others refused. When one of Metacomet's advisors was hung for murder in 1675, the sachem's braves went on
the warpath in a widespread campaign against fifty-two communities across New England. This wasn't reactionary but a
response long in coming, with a clear rationale that Philip articulated at the outset of the conflict:

> The English who came first to this country were but a
> handful of people, forlorn, poor and distressed. My father
> was then sachem. He relieved their distresses in the most
> kind and hospitable manner. He gave them land to plant
> and build upon . . . They flourished and increased . . . By

various means they got possessed of a great part of his territory. But he still remained their friend till he died. My elder brother became sachem. They pretended to suspect him of evil designs against them. He was seized and confined and thereby thrown into illness and died. Soon after I became sachem, they disarmed all my people . . . Their lands were taken . . . But a small part of the dominion of my ancestors remains. I am determined not to live until I have no country.[26]

Instead of letting his country slip away, King Philip fought for it. Every town west of Concord was torched. It was as if hostile Natives had risen from the swamps. Robert Blood's growing estate would be at the epicenter of a violent conflict that spared no man, woman, or child.

Just a mile from Blood Farm's westerly border was the settlement of Nashoba. These were "praying Indians," a tribe that had been successfully converted to Christianity by zealot Puritan minister the Reverend John Eliot under the Act for the Propagation of the Gospel Amongst the Indians, passed by the General Court in 1646. Bound by a common spiritual vision, "praying Indians" were supposed to be the allies of the settlers, and they often were. But as Metacomet's Revenge—as the war was often called—began to threaten the town of Concord, its residents came to doubt the good intentions of these new converts.[27] Robert Blood's father-in-law was assigned the task of overseeing the activities of the Nashoba tribe and guarding against nighttime raids. It was agreed: the only way to effectively guarantee the safety of Concord was to bring the community at Nashoba into the town limits and place a curfew on their "guests." Willard was initially lenient in his policies toward the tribe, urging restraint and arguing against an idea held by many colonists that Native peoples should be sold into slavery and shipped to Barbados. Willard prevailed on this point but failed to assuage his neighbors' worries. In many respects, slavery would have been preferable to the fate that befell them. In the dead of winter, the Natives were marched under armed guard from Concord to Boston.[28]

The Puritans had been exiled from the islands of Great Britain, and in a predictable if ironic turn, used the fear of ostracism to control their fledgling settlements. Nonconformists were called "troublesome." They were unwelcome; it was as simple as that. The Puritans, the pariahs of England, had become masters of banishment. Boston was no place for Native people, even praying ones, during King Philip's War. On the docks of Boston Harbor, Willard looked on as rowboats were filled with the families who once lived on the Concord River.[29] They were cold and hungry even before they set off. Things got significantly worse when they were dropped off on Deer Island, in the middle of the harbor. It was one of America's first internment camps, the temporary home of between five hundred and a thousand Natives forced to subsist on clams. Clamshells were wampum, or money, for these Natives, but the fleshy insides of the bivalves dredged from sandy mud are notoriously dirty and, in this case, responsible for countless "fluxes" and diseases. When spring came, only three hundred imprisoned Natives had survived the tortures and trauma of Deer Island.[30]

There would be a modicum of comfort in thinking that Robert Blood followed his father-in-law in speaking on behalf of the Natives of Nashoba and the surrounding area, but this desire for moral ease almost certainly runs counter to the facts.

In the area surrounding Concord, it was legal, if not expected, to shoot on sight any Native walking by himself, and summary execution of Native men and women was de rigueur. The aptly named English captain Henchman reported that during an expedition six miles north of Blood Farm "eleven [Indians] we had in all, two of whom by council we put to death."[31] The "council" was, at best, perfunctory. In Hadley, Massachusetts, the bloodshed was even more indiscriminate: a Native woman was seized and "it was ordered that she was to be torn to pieces by Doggs, and she was soe dealt with."[32] The antagonism went both ways: on February 12, 1676, Mary Shepherd was abducted by men of the Wampanoag three miles from Robert Blood's homestead. Her two brothers, Jacob and Isaac, who were threshing grain in a nearby field, were brutally murdered. Mary was taken fifty miles south to Braintree, where she managed to escape and returned home to alert men, like Robert Blood, of the attack.

Robert, however, would not have needed such notice, and his animosity toward the Indigenous people of the area could have only deepened in the coming month when a band of King Philip's warriors, led by Monaco, also known as One-Eyed John of the Nipmucks, razed Groton. On the eve of the attack, Robert was in possession of twenty acres of Groton land, just to the northwest of Blood Farm; his brother Richard held the largest grant in the community, with sixty acres; his brother-in-law, Samuel Willard, was the minister in town; his father-in-law inhabited a Groton farmhouse that served as the meeting place for government officials and military commanders. On the evening of March 2, 1676, Simon Willard's house was the first to be burned to the ground. At dawn, when the smoke cleared, the

Natives were gone but the number of standing homes in Groton had been cut in half. A week later the attackers returned: a Native lookout was spotted on a hill above town. Immediately the colonial soldiers, including the Bloods, stationed at one of Groton's four garrisoned houses struck out to capture the lone Native adversary.[33] They had walked right into a trap: the lookout wasn't alone. Reaching the top of the hill, the colonists were ambushed—one was killed, two were badly wounded, several were captured (including Blood), and the rest were forced to flee to another garrison at the very edge of the settlement. Here they looked on as One-Eyed John's men set the rest of their town ablaze. All the while, the Native leader sat outside the garrison, taunting the soldiers and promising the destruction of communities to the south: Chelmsford, Billerica, and Concord, the villages that abutted Blood Farm. Richard Blood's farm at Groton was completely destroyed in the raid, his family forced to flee south, through Blood Farm, to the temporary safety of Concord and Boston.[34]

Following the devastation wrought at Groton, Robert Blood's mood could have been nothing but unforgiving and dour. On March 12, writing from Boston, Increase Mather reported that "this week one who was taken captive at Groton escaped from the Enemy's hands. His name is Blood, a troublesome man in that place! I wish the return of such a man to us may not be ominous of a return of Blood."[35] This "troublesome man" could have been either Robert, John, or Richard, but in any case, Mather's "trouble," which he had foreseen in 1673, was now very near indeed and embodied in the ambition and the unruliness of the Bloods. For the time being, however, the trouble would be quelled, because in the spring of 1676, the family abandoned their homes on Blood Farm and took up residence at Concord with the hope that a critical mass of soldiers would deter future attacks. The Bloods had, at least temporarily, become townspeople.

IN THE SPRINGTIME, the lands once owned by Robert Blood still awaken with a quiet glory and invite freedoms that are not to be squandered—to watch the dew glisten and dry in the morning sun, to surprise a clutch of red-winged blackbirds in the reeds, to walk through orchards of wild apples at the edges of swamps teeming with life, to lie in the grass and make like a log (which is what Thoreau loved to do in the Bloods' pastures). As the ground thaws and the snow melts, rivulets widen, deepen, and the gurgling of water becomes the aural background of everyday life. In 1660, Robert Blood had erected a sawmill driven by these erratic waters, a mill that supplied his family and his neighbors with lumber. When summer approached, the pastures drained, exposing black loam that immediately gave rise to new seedlings. The American Bloods were, at least at first, subsistence farmers, but in a land like this, subsistence occasionally gave way to sheer bounty. Perfect self-sufficiency, the ability to be entirely self-reliant, might be practically impossible, but on Blood Farm, at the height of spring, it seemed more than plausible. In the 1850s, the author and journalist Franklin Sanborn was invited to visit Blood Farm and he reflected that to be such a "borderer" was almost like settling a new colony. There were hardships, undoubtedly many of them, but there were also advantages and, above all, liberties.[36]

Liberty is precisely what the Bloods had to give up in the turmoil of King Philip's War. In fleeing to the protective realm of Concord, Robert Blood forfeited the freedoms he had enjoyed in return for a modicum of safety. This, according to Thomas Hobbes's pessimistic vision, was how civil society was born: in the desperate attempt to quash fear. "The original of all great and lasting societies," Hobbes wrote, just years before King Philip's rise, "consists not in the mutual good will men had toward each other, but of the mutual fear they had of each other."[37] With an enemy at the gates, Hobbes explains, "there is no man who can hope by his own strength or wit to defend himself from destruction without the help of confederates; where every one expects the same defense by the confederation that any one else does; and therefore he which declares he thinks it reason to deceive those that help him can in reason expect no other means of safety than what can be had from his own single power."[38] Many colonists died during King Philip's War (although many more Native Americans did) and the population that survived coalesced in city centers. Concord, for instance, lost one-sixth of its men during the conflict, yet managed to increase its population significantly by receiving refugees from burned-out towns like Groton and Dunstable.

The fear and hatred that came to the fore in King Philip's War had what for Hobbes would have been a predictable effect—it drew English frontiersmen living on the periphery back to the commons. These forces, as Jill Lepore explains, simultaneously forged the hard core of modern American identity: selfhood in the fledgling nation was defined against the backdrop of "the other," the savage, the Native.[39] Settlements like Concord maintained, and in some cases regained, their exceptional status in this crisis; they were regarded as near holy places for the simple reason that they provided rare safe havens from the godless horde that threatened to emerge with torches and tomahawks in the night. Survival and victory for the colonists was interpreted in exclusively theological, if not messianic, terms. In Increase Mather's words, "God has wasted the Heathen by sending the destroying Angell among them since the War began."[40] Of course it wasn't nearly as simple as this.

In 1676, it was not clear that "the Heathen" had lost or that God was actually on the colonists' side. As hostilities began to cool in the southern theater of New England, there was still the desperate sense among Puritan leaders that the Indigenous people had to be made into something less than human, satanic beings that could set English colonial piety in stark relief. The city on a hill needed a border. Its inhabitants needed an enemy. It wasn't enough, for example, that Metacomet was shot and killed in August 1676 by a Native *praying* in a swamp outside Bristol, Rhode Island. Not nearly enough. His head had to be severed and placed on a pike that was paraded into Plymouth Colony, where it remained for twenty years; his body was diced into pieces and hung in the local trees; his hand was delivered to his killer as a trophy. This macabre demonstration was meant to put an end to the Native leader, but it had something of the opposite effect. Metacomet was made out to be so diabolically evil that he robustly lived on after death, haunting settler communities for years to come, giving rise to the conviction that the colonists had to remain vigilant, dedicated, always on guard. The cultivation of fear—the replaying and recollecting of existential crises—helped solidify the political commitments of many townspeople in the early American colonies. It was best to stay at home, close to your neighbor—to circle the proverbial wagons. Woe to those who failed to do so.

The fears in Concord, however, did subside ever so slightly in the fall of 1676 after Metacomet's death, and even more so after the Treaty of Casco brought King Philip's War to an official

end in 1678. Robert Blood now had a choice: ally himself permanently with Concord or return to Blood Farm. He had, in
a moment of panic, entered into a tacit agreement with the
settlement—he was a soldier of Concord during the war and
received his pay through the town; during the war he abided
by the laws of the township and gave up many liberties, most
notably by paying town and ecclesiastical rates, what today we
call taxes. In return, he and his family received the security that
only a functioning town government could provide. But now, in
a time of relative peace, the liberties of Blood Farm beckoned
yet again. Hobbes understood what Blood's turning his back on
Concord might mean, writing in *Leviathan*:

> He . . . that breaketh his covenant, and consequently de-
> clareth that he thinks he may with reason do so, cannot be
> received into any society, that unite themselves for peace
> and defence . . . nor when he is received, be retained in it
> without seeing the danger of their error; which errors a
> man cannot reasonably reckon upon as the means of his
> security; and therefore if he be left, or cast out of society, he
> perisheth; and if he live in society, it is by the errors of other
> men, which he could not foresee, nor reckon upon; and
> consequently against the reason of his preservation; and
> so, as all men that contribute not to his destruction, forbear
> him only out of ignorance of what is good for themselves.[41]

Increase Mather was right: Blood was a troublesome man.
He returned to his independent fiefdom outside the city limits
as soon as the imminent threat was over. He simply didn't want
or need neighbors who weren't his immediate kin. In the 1670s,
two hundred yards from Wolf Rock, the Carlisle Bloods had

helped construct a fortress on a rocky hillside that would become known by locals as "the city," a place where anyone could
take refuge in the event of renewed hostilities with the Natives.
At the time, entrenchments had been dug through the swamps
and lined with bricks as defenses against attack. In 1687, however, Robert and his son Josiah went further: they built a proper
garrison at Blood Farm that still stands to this day. A portion
of the structure was constructed of brick, a material rarely
used in seventeenth-century Massachusetts. Fifteen feet above
ground, in the brick-lined end wall, were ports for muskets.[42]
Every functioning principality possesses means of security but
also infrastructure: Robert's land was indispensable to Concord
and Boston given that the road that crossed Old North Bridge
at James Blood's soon-to-be manse ran directly through Blood
Farm and was one of the very few arteries that connected these
communities to the northern districts and "upper towns" of
New England. This is not to say that the road was anywhere
near smooth or well-defined, but it was still a road, and Robert
Blood was largely responsible for its maintenance.

Many families that owned land in the border country of
New England didn't actually live there. They were land speculators, waiting for civilization to catch up to their expansive
claims. In the meantime, they hunted, farmed, felled trees, and
quarried stone exactly where they pleased without interference
from colonial authorities. The towns nearby did not take kindly
to this practice or to the idea that these settlers could amass a
fortune that was functionally untaxed. On October 11, 1682,
the General Court of Massachusetts declared it to be a grievance that "sundry Gentlemen, merchants, and other" own
great and profitable expanses on the outskirts of the colonies yet
contributed nothing to the commonwealth.[43] It was determined

that these individuals were to pay two shillings annually for every hundred acres in their possession. The new law was not directed at the Bloods—they weren't merely speculating at life—but it was to affect them all the same. The Blood family name had come into being four hundred years earlier with the English institution of taxes on the Scottish border; in other words, the family had come into existence in tandem with the expansion of state powers. Now, on the American frontier, Robert would make a decision regarding the Bloods' relationship with the new seat of government. It was decided: the Bloods would not pay a cent.

FROM ROBERT'S PERSPECTIVE, the land tax must have been especially objectionable. The Bloods had reluctantly—occasionally—paid ecclesiastical dues first to Billerica and then to Concord, but they would also occasionally attend church, both in Billerica and in Concord. Not all the time—the trip was long and hard—but often enough to satisfy Elizabeth Willard, who undoubtedly wanted to go more than Robert (Elizabeth's brother Samuel was the preacher in Groton and would later take over Harvard College when Increase Mather was ousted by the trustees). The land tax, by contrast, seemed without cause and exorbitant. By that time, the Bloods had amassed more than 2,500 acres of land, bringing the corresponding tax to three British pounds. At that time, builders and farmers, on average, earned between ten and fifteen pounds a year, so this was not a trivial sum, and would be added to the municipal and church dues that were already owed each year. Blood's taxes went unpaid for two years, until Concord constables, armed with the appropriate tax warrants, crossed the town boundary and made for Robert Blood's farmhouse between Punkatasset Hill, also known as Indian Hill, and Tophet Swamp. The constables also brought a posse. Robert and his sons, Robert Jr. and Simon, met the tax collectors at the front door.

By some accounts, the constables were met with "contumelious speeches" but, more pivotally, with "actual violence to their persons."[44] It seems the Bloods roundly pounded the men from Concord. In the coming months Robert would be fined ten pounds (nearly a full year's wage) for abusing Constable John Wheeler, who was regarded by many as rivaling Simon Willard for the title of the most respectable man in the Concord area. Robert Jr. was ordered to give bond for good behavior. Blood retaliated by suing Wheeler for accosting him "with a great attendance," and "striking him at his own house," but it appears that Blood was the only one who had to pay damages.[45] This reprimand would have been enough to teach most people

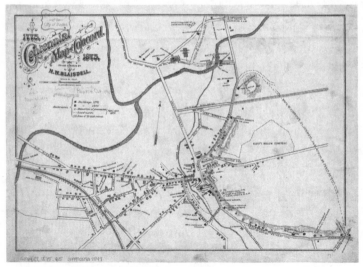

Map of Concord, Massachusetts

a lesson, but the Bloods weren't most people. The following
year, Robert and his two sons were again arraigned on charges
of "disorderly carnage" against town officials seeking to collect
their "just rates." Between the years 1680 and 1711, there were
fewer than thirty litigated assaults in the courts of Middlesex
County (less than one a year). The Bloods were responsible for
two of them.[46]

The confrontation between Robert Blood and the Concord magistrates hints at allegory and presages in miniature
the political dynamics that quickly came to dominate Colonial America first in the 1680s and then, once again, as the
country descended into revolution. In the year that Blood was
brought to trial for his abusing of the tax collectors, the colonial administration of Massachusetts came to defy the English
Crown, a centralized power they could not abide. More specifically, beginning with the Restoration of Charles II in 1660,
Puritan leaders refused to recognize that the king had any authority over the governance of colonies. The colonies were to
be run independently. The Crown had other ideas: on June 18,
1684, James II, who had assumed the throne after the death of
his brother, formally revoked the colony's charter.

Just as Robert Blood was stiffly fined for beating Constable
Wheeler, the Puritans were made to pay for their outsized sense
of liberty and entitlement. James II placed the colony under
royal authority, creating the Dominion of New England, administered by Sir Edmund Andros, a staunch Royalist and de-
fender of the Anglican Church. The Puritans were essentially
cut out of the political life of the American colonies: Andros
was to govern with a council composed of representatives from
across the northern colonies, but due to the cost and difficulty

of travel, the advisors of the new Dominion were largely hand-picked by Andros himself. In his first months in office, he turned his attention to reforming the religious framework of the settle-ment, requesting and then demanding a space to hold Anglican services. The clergy of Boston refused the man they called a "bigoted Papist," but Andros set his sights on one congrega-tion: the Third Church of Boston, led by Samuel Willard, the brother-in-law of Robert Blood.[47] When Andros expressed his intentions to take over Willard's church, the laymen of the con-gregation furnished the governor a deed that stated clearly that the building was privately owned and could, therefore, not be seized by the Crown. Private property was not to be confiscated without an owner's permission. With an owner's permission, it wasn't called confiscation at all; rather, it was a sale or inheri-tance. None of this mattered to Andros. The king had to be satisfied. The sexton of Third Church was commanded to open the doors to Anglicans on Good Friday 1687. Just to avoid any confusion, the command was accompanied with a reminder of what could happen to Protestants who refused to obey such orders: the French Huguenots had been massacred only years before when they had attempted to defy the monarchy.

The loss of the charter, and the subsequent undermining of Puritan religious dominion, was a severe blow to the political and cultural institutions of Colonial America. James II was the new, or renewed, ruler, and to make matters worse, he was a recent convert to the Roman Catholicism of his Italian wife, which was abhorrent to the Reformed Christians of Massachu-setts. The crisis of King Philip's War was conjoined with that of the English Civil War. In the turmoil, however, one frontiers-man managed to eke out a marginally respectable reputation.

Robert Blood turned out to be the lesser of two evils: tied closely to the esteemed Willards, he seems to have been forgiven his trespasses and his family was reintegrated into Concord society. Magistrates in the New World would need settlers like Blood in the fight they could sense was looming ahead.

As tensions mounted between the Puritan leaders and Governor Andros, the political situation deteriorated in Great Britain. James II had tended toward Catholicism for many years, but when he sired a Catholic heir, many Protestant nobles had had enough: they invited William III of Orange and his wife and first cousin, Mary II, to assume the throne. William III headed a fleet from Holland and invaded England in 1688; James II fled and was assumed to have abdicated. This bloodless coup, this Glorious Revolution, rippled through the empire. Massachusetts was quick to feel its effects: in April 1689, the militia from Concord joined two thousand colonial soldiers and marched on Boston, first arresting the captain of the British ship *Rose*, docked in Boston Harbor, and then imprisoning Andros, who remained incarcerated for more than a year. Leading the Concord soldiers was Lt. John Heald, patriarch of the other large family that resided near the Bloods along the town's northern frontier. "We have been quiet, hitherto," the leaders of the revolt explained, "but now the Lord has prospered the undertaking of the prince of Orange, we think we should follow such an example. We therefore, seized the vile persons who oppressed us."[48] Good government did not turn on security alone, but also on the ability to exercise one's rights and liberties under the law. In the absence of this ability, one was justified in fighting to reclaim it.

Increase Mather might have become the spokesman for the colonial cause in the conflict, which came to be known as the Boston Revolt, but he was away in England, attempting to negotiate a new charter as tensions were drawn to a breaking point. In his absence, it was Samuel Willard, Elizabeth Blood's brother, who became the standard-bearer of Puritan rectitude against Andros's Anglicanism and the king's Catholicism. Not only did Willard maintain the traditional fasting days at Third Church after Andros forbade them—this was the sort of non-conformity that Puritans could applaud—but, more importantly, he sustained an almost superhuman program of pastoral care through the last two decades of the eighteenth century. If there was a sick boy in Roxbury or a dying woman on Beacon Hill, Willard was there. He was seen by many of his contemporaries as an angel of justice and mercy. In short, Willard embodied John Winthrop's initial ideological mandate for the colonies. As Ebenezer Pemberton claimed in his funeral sermon for Willard in 1707, "He knew how to be a Son of Thunder to the Secure and Hardened and the Son of Consolation to the Contrite and Broken in Spirit."[49] It is difficult to imagine that Willard's popularity didn't have a significant knock-on effect on his sister's family's standing in the Massachusetts community.

AT THE AGE of fifty-five, in 1690, Elizabeth Willard Blood died. Married to a man of the wilderness whose ambition was rivaled only by his temper, she could not have lived the life she had once envisioned as a wealthy girl raised in Concord, but there may have been many loving moments—brutal rulers often have tender family lives—and the couple produced twelve children, most of whom watched their own children and children's children grow up on Blood Farm. Elizabeth is, most likely, buried somewhere on the south side of Tophet Swamp, on the higher ground where she and Robert once had their main farmhouse. After the death of his wife, it seems that Robert's temper cooled significantly. He started paying his taxes regularly to Concord, at least in part because the town appears to have eased its policy toward Blood Farm: in 1696, land taxes were reduced; the Bloods were occasionally exempted from certain duties of public office (Robert didn't want them); and the nonarable land of Blood Farm was exempted from ministerial dues. It is very likely that after the Boston Revolt of 1689, however, Blood and the residents of Concord had reached a much deeper philosophical pact. They had come to agree on what philosophers of the time termed "the right of revolution."

The Glorious Revolution that swept through the British Isles in 1688 and 1689 was ushered in by a radical transition in political philosophy overseen by the English philosopher and physician John Locke, a man who today is regarded as the "Father of Liberalism." Born in 1632, to a father who fought in the Parliamentary army against Charles I in the English Civil War, Locke was, almost from birth, an enemy of the Crown. Locke's mature political thought was not written directly in support of William III—as it is sometimes thought—but it was wholly in agreement with the ethos of his new authority. Locke argued against absolute monarchy in all its forms, both in the patriarchal rule of Filmer and the *Leviathan* of Hobbes. The monarchists believed that a king's authority could not be challenged under any circumstances, but Locke suggested that recent events had proven that the costs of such a position were simply too high, writing in *The Second Treatise of Civil Government*:

> For when the *People* are made *miserable*, and find themselves
> *exposed to the ill usage of Arbitrary Power*, cry up their Gover-

nours, as much as you will for Sons of *Jupiter*, let them be
Sacred and Divine, descended or authoriz'd from Heaven;
give them out for whom or what you please, the same will
happen. *The People generally ill treated*, and contrary to right,
will be ready upon any occasion to ease themselves of a
burden that sits heavy upon them.[50]

Ill-treated people will rightly overthrow their oppressors.
Like Hobbes, Locke was a contractarian, but he held that a
government must be responsive, much more responsive, to the
particular needs of its citizens, in order to earn its legitimacy.
It was not enough for a king to protect his realm from invasion, and to use the same methods of deterrence to petrify his
subjects into submission. Instead, the legitimacy of political authority turned on a sovereign's willingness to respect what philosophers after Locke would commonly call "natural rights"; for
Locke, these included the "life, liberty, and property (estate)" of
an individual living under the social contract. Indeed, these are
the same rights that Thomas Blood, the jewel thief, appealed
to in his defense before Charles II: his rights had been compromised in Ireland in the English Civil War and therefore he was
forced to steal the Crown. By the same token, Locke argued,
when the natural rights of a group of able-bodied individuals
were violated by the state, a sovereign could expect his citizens
to rise against him or her.

On December 16, 1689, Locke's theoretical model for natural rights was put into practical effect in the English Bill of
Rights. Given the intimate relationship between the Glorious
Revolution and the Boston Revolt, colonial leaders would have
been fully aware of this Act of Parliament that prohibited the
unlawful taxation and incarceration of citizens but also limited

royal authority over free speech and religious practices. Monarchs were no longer just accountable to God; now the people could take them to task. When William and Mary came to power, they had to take the Coronation Oath to "promise and swear to govern the people of this kingdom of England, and the dominions thereunto belonging, according to the statutes in parliament agreed on." They could rule, but only if they did so in accord with the laws of the land.[51]

One of the foundational insights that can be overlooked in Locke's political philosophy, and in the Bill of Rights, is, in fact, about land—about the nature of land and its ownership. "Life, liberty, and the pursuit of happiness" may be the typical motto of modern liberalism, but in the day of Locke and Robert Blood, land and estate were not to be omitted in the discussion of natural rights. In Locke's *Two Treatises of Government*, first published in 1689 and then making a "great noise" in intellectual centers through the 1690s, he takes on a difficult question: How can one possess or own something like dirt? Land, after all, is just earth, and earth belongs to everyone and no one equally. It is common ground. Private property, therefore, seems to be a contradiction in terms. Locke, however, argued that the nature of land changed by virtue of the work that individuals invested in its cultivation and maintenance. "God gave the World to Men in Common," Locke maintained. "But since he gave it them for their benefit, and the greatest Conveniencies of life they were capable to draw from it, it cannot be supposed he meant it should always remain common and uncultivated. He gave it to the use of the industrious."[52] A plot of ground—owned by no one—becomes a farmer's garden, becomes lawful property, when a man or woman spends the time and effort to weed it, hoe it, seed it, and harvest it. Once this act of investing in the land has been made, it must be accounted for in maintenance of a social contract; in other words, a governing body does not have the license to take the land by force or tax it unfairly. Locke explains that "the reason why men enter into society is the preservation of their property," and "government has no other end than the preservation of property."[53] This comment regarding the primacy of property applied to an individual's estate—like Robert Blood's farm—but also to his or her body or basic personhood (this too, for Locke, was property). A government that succeeds in preserving property is worthy of respect and obedience, but one that fails in this basic obligation is no government at all and should be wiped away in the right of rebellion.

In the 1690s, Robert Blood and the Concord magistrates seem to have reached an agreement on this particular philosophical position: they could both be satisfied with the mutual benefits of Locke's social contract. Blood Farm became, at least nominally, part of Concord.[54] Blood's pastures were bountiful and were taxed reasonably. In the twilight of his life, Robert could have looked back and agreed with Locke: "All wealth is the product of labor." His sons and daughters erected homesteads along the choicest stretches of the Concord River. When the time came in the 1750s, Robert's progeny helped establish the district of Carlisle, which became Concord's sister town in 1805. There would occasionally be a quarrelsome sister, but the Bloods would, at least for the time being, run cooler. Robert died in 1701 and his descendants became obedient colonists, or as obedient as any American colonists were in the coming century. Granted, they weren't always wholly cooperative and even as late as 1744 were called (and refused) to perambulate the boundaries of the farm with Concord officials—a yearly ritual that continues to this day in mid-April, when property owners check the rock walls at the edges of their properties.[55] At least the Bloods no longer fought with the constables from Concord. Instead, by the late 1600s, it was agreed that in return for the Bloods' taxes, the town of Concord would construct and maintain two roads that ran from Old North Bridge to Blood Farm. The first was a cart path, thirty feet wide (two rods), known as Two Rod Road, the second a parallel thruway, called Estabrook Road.

In the mist of early morning on April 19, 1775, twenty-one men, between the ages of nineteen and fifty-four, met at the edge of Blood Farm.[56] They had been called by the beating of a drum moments before, and had gathered in a bit more than a minute. The trip to Old North Bridge would be just under five

British March, April 19, 1775

miles. They would meet the redcoats there. Estabrook was, according to legend, the route. Tradition says they marched, but at a certain point they might have broken into a run, with rifles in hand—to protect Concord, to steel their country against the Crown, to defend the right of revolution. And an American Blood was already there, waiting to join them.

PART II

LIBERTY

THE MINUTEMAN

What could the body of freemen, meeting four times a year, at Boston, do for the daily wants of the planters at Musketaquid? The wolf was to be killed; the Indian to be watched and resisted; wells to be dug; the forest to be felled; pastures to be cleared; corn to be raised; roads to be cut; town and farm lines to be run. These things must be done, govern who might. The nature of man and his condition in the world, for the first time within the period of certain history, controlled the formation of the State.

—RALPH WALDO EMERSON,
HISTORICAL DISCOURSES AT CONCORD, 1835[1]

IT WAS 1833, AND RALPH WALDO EMERSON, AFTER many years, had come home to Concord. The town was two hundred years old and Emerson was invited to give the commemorating address, to explain how colonial freemen, bound to England, had eventually set America loose upon the world. In advance of the address, Emerson undertook something he rarely did—he actually prepared. He scoured the historical

documents of the town and its border regions, and he interviewed the elderly inhabitants who could still remember a time
when liberty was not secure. Emerson's lecture would be something more than a simple historical study. It would, at its best,
tap into the singular, but universal, character of the American
experience: Emerson wanted to give his audience a sense of
revolution from within but also convey its transcendent nature.
He wanted to do nothing less than to capture the experience
and spirit of revolution.

The Revolution, for Emerson and those who would become
his fellow transcendentalists, had to be immediate, ongoing,
indefinite. In his commemorative lecture, he was after the subjective sense of radical transformation, the personal risks and
possibilities of nonconformity. Indeed, that would become his
enduring intent—the intellectual battle cry for which he would
become known as the "sage of Concord." The lecture of 1835
presented a challenge. If Emerson wanted to understand the
most pivotal moment of American history, Concord's claim to
fame, the best he could do, since he hadn't actually been there,
was talk to a man who had been. There was only one problem.
The minutemen who fought at the Battle of Old North Bridge
were all dead. Except one. So Emerson sought out the last minuteman: a man by the name of Thaddeus Blood.

Emerson arranged the meeting. It was virtually the first
thing he did upon putting down roots in Concord. On July 30,
he left his new home, Bush, and his family home, the Old
Manse, and disappeared into Estabrook Woods to the north of
town. He had an appointment to keep. He most likely climbed
Punkatasset Hill, cut west a quarter of a mile, and north again
through Mason's Pasture, catching Two Rod Road. The red
buds of the mountain laurel would have opened, marking the

fields with outcroppings of their white flowers, creating the perfect setting for the budding transcendentalist to do his historical
research.[2]

Emerson had—in a moment of questionable judgment—
invited his step-grandfather, Dr. Ezra Ripley, to join him. He
would come to regret that decision. Ripley was the "old oak" of
the Concord community, nearly eighty-six at the time, and the
last guardian of the town's Puritanical past. Perhaps Emerson
thought that Ripley's age would put the former soldier, Blood,
at ease, that the two old men could reminisce about the war
freely and give a young nonconformist some insight into the
workings of the world. It didn't turn out that way. Emerson
and Ripley were both interested in the Revolution, but in very

Ralph Waldo
Emerson

different ways. Emerson wanted to reclaim and embody its un-
finished ideals; Ripley just wanted to repeat and embalm the
sacred stories of the past.[3]

Emerson and Ripley passed through the Cedar Swamp
that would, in wet months, drain into the Tophet. John Thoreau, Henry David's father, might have been in the process of
felling some of these trees; he operated the sawmill that the two
men passed on their left. They were almost there. This land,
once called "the Farm," had only recently been fully annexed
to Concord. The last minuteman, thanks to his participation
in the Revolution, was no longer an "outliver," but he still lived
on the edge of civilized life. Here it was: this was the farmhouse
of Thaddeus Blood.

THADDEUS BLOOD was born on May 28, 1755, in a Geor-
gian farmhouse on the edge of the Tophet Swamp, on the banks
of the Concord River, at the boundary of Concord and Carlisle.
In other words, he was born in *our* house—the one that Kath,
the kids, and I now call home. It is very likely that he was born
in the very center of our house, next to the hearth where I first
found *The Story of the Bloods*.[4]

Thaddeus's father, Josiah, great-grandson of Robert (the
settler) and Elizabeth Willard Blood, constructed the house in
1745, in the year of his marriage to Sarah Blood, and he set up a
two-hundred-acre farm that stretched down to the river, where
an ancient Native American settlement had once stood. This
was the site of Thaddeus's childhood. He must have felt like the
chosen son: his four older brothers had all died in infancy before
he had been born. He was the great-great-grandson of the origi-

nal Blood settler, Robert, and his family lived a mile from Robert and Elizabeth's first homestead, a half mile from the onetime home of his grandfather John. Thaddeus was, from the outset, surrounded by an immense family, a legion of relations that did not fit the standard categories of modern kinship. Susannah Blood, a contemporary of Thaddeus, was born a Blood, married twice, and died a Blood, but her name was never anything other than Blood: she married her first cousin, and when he died, she married her other first cousin.[5] Within a century, possibly five different Josiah Bloods (who were not his father), from three different generations, built houses near Thaddeus's. Over the years, Blood Farm had become almost crowded.

By the time Emerson and Ripley came to visit Thaddeus in the summer of 1835, he had moved to another farmhouse in easy shooting distance from his childhood home. He was eighty-six years old, unsteady on his feet, and easily overwhelmed. He could scarcely remember his childhood on the river, but that hardly mattered to his visitors. They were in search of one story. Emerson—as was his wont—wanted to ease into the conversation, to let his elderly interlocutor talk at will, to simply listen. Ripley, however, was not of this mind. Ripley wanted to confirm certain peculiarities about the Concord battle, to jog the old codger's memory, to flush out the truth (just as long as the truth conformed with Ripley's understanding of the event). In his journal, Emerson reflected on the conversation, which, thanks to Ripley, turned into a verbal assault:

> It is affecting to see the old man's [Thaddeus Blood] memory taxed for facts occurring 60 years ago at Concord fight.
> "It is hard to bring them up"; he says . . . Doctor Ripley,

like a keen hunter, unrelenting, follows him up and down,
barricading him with questions. Yet cares little for the
facts the man can tell but much for the confirmation of the
printed history.[6]

Like Robert Blood, Thaddeus seemed to fit an exact model
plucked from American iconography, that of the sturdy freedom
fighter. But Emerson heard something else in his account, something that defied, or at least expanded, Ripley's expectations.
Blood's history was fallible, fragile, and therefore real. In the
"Concord Hymn," Emerson's impressionistic vignette of the
battle, delivered in 1837, two years after his conversation with
Blood, he wrote:

> *By the rude bridge that arched the flood,*
> *Their flag to April's breeze unfurled,*
> *Here once the embattled farmers stood,*
> *And fired the shot heard round the world.*[7]

Thaddeus Blood heard this first shot; in Emerson's words
from the 1835 address, he "saw the water struck by the first
ball."[8] And he was the last man alive to remember it. It was a
"shot heard round the world," but in Emerson's day, this echoing sound had come to mean very different things to different
people. When asked by Ripley what *actually* happened on that
fateful day in April 1775, Blood hesitated and then seized up
completely: "The truth will never be known," he lamented, according to Emerson.[9] The confidence and bravado of youth had
been tempered, and what once might have seemed clear about
the Revolution, or about the battle, had faded for Blood. His
reticence to answer Ripley may have been a sign of confusion

or dementia—or simple annoyance—but Emerson's account of the conversation seems to gesture to another, more meaningful possibility: Thaddeus Blood's recollection of the pursuit of liberty may have led him to dwell on moments when this pursuit faltered or was compromised by cowardice and short-sightedness. The conversation with Ripley and Emerson ended abruptly, even mournfully. "Leave me. Leave me to repose," Blood said.[10]

THE BLOODS DID NOT disdain the prospects of material wealth or worldly pursuits. According to the 1717 assessor's list, the oldest record of its kind in the town of Concord, Thaddeus's uncle was arguably the wealthiest man in Concord.[11] Born of relative privilege, the fourteen-year-old Thaddeus might have had only a vague inkling of the broader political situation that he, his family, and their neighbors would face in the coming decade. Blood Farm in Thaddeus's day was dotted with taverns and inns that welcomed teams of oxen on their way to and from Boston, offering drivers and farmhands glasses of rye for three cents a shot. In the 1760s, young Thaddeus grew up a half mile up the hill from Stephen Blood's Black Mansion, so called because it was so dilapidated and worn that its rough-hewn boards were already, in the mid-1700s, a pitch umber.[12] Stephen, probably Thaddeus's uncle, made a modest fortune—either from the tavern or, more likely, from his profitable asparagus farm nestled on the banks of the Concord River. When the marshy ground thawed in the spring and the plants awoke from their dormancy, the lattice of roots buried in Blood's fields drove the small green spikes toward the skies at the rate of four inches a day. The long summer days were spent harvesting and selling the crop. The long winter nights were spent in front of the giant hearth at the Black Mansion. When that fire ran cold, thirsty patrons could shuffle through the snow, down Bedford Road, to the giant house of Elenathan Blood, which was also used as a tavern. It was said that the Bloods "drank" but not immoderately; they were respectable, but not *that* respectable.[13]

Thaddeus, then, came of age in choice circumstances. His existence as a young man was largely one of his own choosing, an ostensibly free life, embodying a balance between the socially responsible liberties of his ancestor James, the freeman of Concord, and the wild opportunities of Robert, the radically free man of Blood Farm. These old American Bloods represented two archetypes of freedom that would be enshrined in modern political theory, most notably by Isaiah Berlin in 1958 in his essay "Two Concepts of Liberty." Berlin argued that there are two distinct, but interlocking, visions of freedom, what he terms "positive liberty" and "negative liberty." Positive liberty is the freedom expressed in the statement "I am my own master"—I am in charge of my destiny, of the projects and pursuits that I undertake. It is a "freedom to," to participate, to work, to converse, to play, to build, to reflect, to live. In laying claim to positive liberty, one comes to possess the enabling conditions to thrive and flourish on one's own account.[14] Oftentimes positive liberty is understood as a type of open engagement— political, religious, and cultural—that makes a person's life what it is. This was the freedom of James Blood, the freeman, the bedrock of the Concord community. By contrast, negative liberty is the freedom expressed in the idea that "no one is my master"—in other words, no one is interfering with my livelihood in a meaningful or significant way.[15] This is a "freedom from," from constraint, from impediment, from obstacles, from the boundaries that might make living one's life harder than it otherwise should be. Robert Blood's desire to remain free from the strictures of Concord and the burdens of taxes was voiced in the name of negative liberty. By 1755, a boy born into Thaddeus Blood's situation was poised to inherit and enjoy both of these quintessential American liberties.

The prosperity enjoyed by many of the earliest American Bloods, however, always came at a price. On April 7, 1755, a month before Thaddeus's birth, his grandfather John invited his sons, Ezra and Josiah (Thaddeus's father), to witness the bill of sale of a "ten year-old Mulatto girl named Dinah."[16] John would sell the girl, but she would stay in the family, being bought by Hannah Blood, Thaddeus's aunt, for forty pounds. Dinah remained on Blood Farm for many years, long enough for Thaddeus to have looked up to, and then down on, her. Before the towns around Concord became known for their fervent abolitionism in the 1850s, they were known, by Dinah and Thomas Farwell and others like them, for their slavery. Farwell, an enslaved African American who lived first in Groton and then in Carlisle on Blood Farm, was also owned by Thaddeus's grandfather.[17]

By the 1750s, the Bloods were not alone in their slaveholding. After King Philip's War it was no longer possible to force the Native people to work on the Yankee farms of Massachusetts and Connecticut. If wealthy landowners wanted a cheap workforce, another solution had to be sought. The farms in the Massachusetts Bay Colony, like the Blood Farm, didn't require the same number of workers as did the tobacco or rice plantations of the southern colonies, but northern farmers were still more than happy to put a handful of enslaved Africans to work in their house or in their fields, a practice that had an obvious practical advantage for families like the Bloods. It was also a marker of wealth: like owning fine clothes or an extra seven oxen (that was roughly the equivalent value of an enslaved African). Boston, the crucible of independence in the American colonies, had the largest slave population in New England and monitored it carefully. Enslaved people had circumscribed rights: they could own certain types of property, sue for their freedom, and testify in court cases. But they couldn't carry canes or sticks, own hogs, purchase goods at market, or walk about the streets on Sundays or at night. Violators would be whipped. Slavery may not have been as deeply entrenched in the cultural and economic institutions of Boston and the surrounding area as in the southern colonies, but it still existed and it supported Thaddeus Blood's family.[18]

Locke's "right of revolution" maps directly onto the story of America, but not in the way that one might like to think. Locke, like many of the political leaders he would later inspire, could not consistently define the practical scope of the analysis. Who exactly deserved liberty, and who did not? That became the question of the New World, and one that Locke failed to answer in any satisfying way. In 1670, Locke drafted the constitution of the new colony of Carolina, and he clearly states that religious differences between settlers and Natives did not justify the ill treatment or oppression of the tribes that coexisted with the European settlements. He also suggested, in a moment of forward thinking, that there are no salient biological differences between the races that would make one man or woman inherently more deserving, or able to exercise, his or her liberty. But when it came to slavery, Locke seems to have sacrificed consistency and justice for convenience and the status quo, writing in the Caro-

lina constitution that "every Freeman of Carolina Shall have
Absolute Power over His Negro Slaves."[19] He never attempted
to justify this claim, but the claim stood nonetheless—as did
Locke's long-standing monetary investment in the Royal African
Company, which helped bring more than ten million Africans to
America during three centuries of active slave trading. These in-
consistencies, at the very heart of modern liberalism and democratic theory, came to define colonial life in the South, but also
quietly infiltrated the lives and beliefs of New Englanders in the
century leading up to the Revolution.

Many leaders of the American Revolution lived out the
radical discontinuity between holding slaves and fighting for a
nation's freedom—the most famous being George Washington,
who has been roundly and rightly criticized for the nearly three
hundred enslaved Black people who worked on his estate in
Mount Vernon and some of whom received their liberty only
after the death of his wife, Martha. The same hypocrisy and
shortsightedness, however, was rampant in New England, not
only in Washington's Virginia: the Reverend William Emerson, who would become a firebrand for the Revolution, owned
Frank, an enslaved man who lived, most likely, in a corner of
the Old Manse. Emerson had every opportunity to discuss the
issue of slavery from the pulpit but the topic is notably absent
from his sermons, which probably had at least something to do
with the inclinations of his congregation. Duncan Ingraham, a
stalwart of the Concord community, trafficked heavily in slaves
before retiring in the shadow of First Church.[20]

While other residents of Concord owned slaves, the Bloods'
participation in the institution appears to have deviated from
the norm in various ways. By many accounts, in 1770, between

eight and thirteen families in Concord owned slaves. The will of Josiah Blood, the wealthy great-grandfather to Thaddeus, dated 1728, states that a sum of one hundred pounds, half of his orchard, and his "negro boy" should be given to his wife, Mary, upon his death.[21] This document indicates that the Bloods were relatively early slave owners in the colony, perhaps one of the very first, especially given John and Josiah's direct descent from the founding American Blood, Robert. If this document creates one historical bookend, it is possible that the account of Dinah provides another. The note regarding the bill of sale of Dinah in 1755 is accompanied by a letter from Thaddeus's cousin saying that he had, in fact, "seen Dinah for many years" after she was passed to Hannah Blood. How many years and in what capacity is unknown. Since slavery officially ended in Massachusetts in 1783, this reference suggests that the Bloods were long-standing stakeholders in the slave trade.

Was the life of an enslaved Black person drastically worse than that of a white bonded laborer in New England in the 1700s? One thing is certain: neither of these groups could exercise positive or negative liberty. In the words of the historian Robert Gross, "Deprived of independence, denied the fruits of their labor, always subject to the will of others, they were living embodiments of what British 'slavery' could mean—models that the whites of Concord [in the Revolution] anxiously struggled to avoid."[22] Though this is true, even this philosophical point risks understating the brutality of New England slavery, or the practices that took place on homesteads like Blood Farm. Before 1740, just north of Blood Farm in the town of Groton—the town that was razed in King Philip's War—lived Robert Blood Jr., a cousin of Josiah. He too owned a slave, whose name has not entered the historical record. Groton had been rebuilt by that time, but there was absolutely no love lost between the tribes living on the New Hampshire border and the Bloods who had taken up residence in Groton, which meant, in lieu of Native laborers, colonists increasingly turned to enslaved Black people as laborers.

The colonial records of Dunstable, a village on the outskirts of Groton, report that at some point in the 1730s Robert Blood Jr. fell extremely ill.[23] He needed medicine that only the Natives of the area could provide, and he visited a Native doctor to procure the concoction. But, given the open animosity between himself and the local tribes, he was hesitant to take the medicine, and forced the enslaved boy to take the elixir first.[24] It turns out that Blood's suspicion was well-founded. The innocent boy died—and was buried on "Negro Hill" just outside of town. Nightshade, which grows like a weed across the wetlands of Massachusetts and Connecticut, can be used as an ointment for abrasions and cuts, but if you consume more than a few berries, you risk permanent paralysis. Water hemlock, readily available in New Hampshire, is basically the same substance that killed Socrates—suddenly, by painful convulsions. Wolfsbane, with its beautiful purple flowers, grows in the high altitudes of the Northeast and is probably the worst: a victim dies by asphyxiation by mere exposure to the plant's drooping foliage. Whatever it was, the innocent and nameless boy perished whereas Robert lived on into his sixties.[25]

As Thaddeus came of age and prepared to join the mounting revolt against Britain, one form of homegrown oppression begat another. And his kinfolk, the American Bloods, survived and thrived. This was now Thaddeus Blood's family: very rich, very free, and complicit in the subjugation of others. The wolf-like tactics of Machiavelli had found a home in the New World.

THIS BRUTAL HISTORY of America was not the story of freedom that the Reverend Ripley wished to discuss with Thaddeus on his visit with Emerson to Blood's house in 1835. Something far more triumphant was expected. Ripley wanted the aged Thaddeus to recount a single morning of heroism, the dawning of a great nation. In a certain respect, it was a reasonable request. Thaddeus had been there, and had been one of few at the time to write about the Concord battle of April 19, 1775. At one point, the elderly man knew well the history of the events he took part in. "The causes which led to hostilities between Great Britain and America are well known, to all those with an acquaintance of history,"[26] he wrote.

Tensions between the colonial leaders and British authorities intensified as Thaddeus entered adulthood. Imperial taxes were no longer mere annoyances; they were odious signs of monarchical overreach that had to be banished as quickly as possible. On December 16, 1773, a group of sixty colonists, dressed as members of the Mohawk tribe, revolted against the Tea Act, passed earlier that year, by pitching 342 cases of tea into Boston Harbor. "The People should never rise, without doing something to be remembered—something notable and striking," John Adams wrote of the Tea Party, continuing, "This Destruction of the Tea is so bold, so daring, so firm, intrepid and inflexible, and it must have so important Consequences, and so lasting, that I can't but consider it as an Epoch in History."[27]

In the prelude to full-scale war, Thaddeus's Concord neighbors were not nearly as intrepid in their defiance of the

Crown. That time would come—and rather quickly—but the Concordians were notably ambivalent and wary when it came to outright dissent. Blood Farm was within the backwater of the backwater of the British Empire. In the 1760s, Concord remained out of the way—possessing virtually none of the commodities that made it strategically valuable to the Crown—and Blood Farm was still on the borderland of the social contract. The best that British authorities could hope for was to extract moneys from these remote outposts in the form of taxes. The Bloods—with their long history of fighting taxes—would have understood, and perhaps resented, these methods of control. The Sugar Act was levied on the colonies in 1764, and the next year the Stamp Act was passed and began to tax basically every scrap of paper in the settlements, from deeds to wills. In the fall of 1765, Concord sent their legislative representative to resist this "burthensome tax."[28] In the end, however, the chosen representative, Charles Prescott, proved reluctant to buck British authority. The inhabitants of Concord might be annoyed by the tariffs, but they would remain content to deal with their own local affairs for the time being, as was certainly the case for the residents of Blood Farm. Relative peace and prosperity has a cloistering, blinkering effect. They'd been relatively slow to entertain the possibility of open conflict with England, which was, even in the lead-up to war, referred to as a "tender parent," but by the spring of 1775 the rumblings of war swept through their town as well. The oxcarts that frequented the Black Mansion from Boston now carried contraband—rice, gun carriages, cannons—and in many cases distributed the goods among the Blood farmhouses. Col. James Barrett, who was appointed as the head of the Concord militia, was responsible for caching supplies at thirty private homes, including the Bloods', across the Merrimack Valley. Historians know this at least in part because Thaddeus Blood wrote it down.

At the age of nineteen, Thaddeus joined Barrett's regiment as a private. In his written account of the Concord fight, Blood explains the buildup to hostilities with surprising sophistication:

> In October 1774, General Gage . . . had dissolved . . . the Court, the greater part of its members met at Salem notwithstanding, and formed themselves into a provincial Congress . . . and adjourned to Concord and chose Mr. Hancock president—they secretly agreed to make preparations to oppose the acts of parliament until we should have redress of the grievances we complained of . . . the Congress recommended the forming of Companies of Minute Men—and the collecting of stores and cannon were collected and deposited in Concord under the superintendence of Col. James Barrett.[29]

General Gage was the British army officer—then governor—charged with the impossible, ill-advised task of subduing a colony that had, by that point, almost decided that it deserved complete self-government. Gage had his commands from George III to execute what came to be known as the Intolerable Acts, the statutes meant to punish Massachusetts after the Boston Tea Party. Gage was also supposed to be the prime beneficiary of the Massachusetts Government Act that was to give the royally appointed governor unprecedented powers over the colonists. This act, however, remained largely inactive—hamstrung by the fact that Gage's actual power did not extend beyond the city limits of Boston. Gage wanted to change that, entreating the Crown to use force, great force, to place

Massachusetts back under royal control: "A large force will ter-rify," Gage explained to his superiors, echoing absolutists like Hobbes, "a middling one will encourage resistance." He was prescient. Perhaps George III should have listened.[30]

The Provincial Congress, led by John Hancock, was in the process of raising an actual army. The plan was almost set: in the second week of April 1775, the Congress authorized the enlisting of eighteen thousand men from across New England. When the Congress recessed on April 15, a spy from Concord informed Gage that this might be the last chance to seize the stockpiles at Lexington and Concord. On April 19, the Brit-ish commander rallied his grenadiers—the special forces of the royal military—and marched west, flashing through Lexington (where they killed eight minutemen in under half an hour), and moved on to Concord, toward the Blood family homesteads.

While the eighty-six-year-old Thaddeus Blood could not give a detailed account of the Concord battle to Ripley and Emerson, he did convey the core of the event, which was cor-roborated by a number of sources and reflected a written state-ment that Blood drafted after the battle, a document that was discovered in the Blood family papers after Thaddeus's death and published in the *Boston Advertiser* on April 20, 1886.[31] On the fateful morning of the battle, at "about 2 o'clock in the morning," Thaddeus Blood wrote, "I was called out of bed by John Barrett, a Sergeant of the militia company to which I be-longed."[32] The British regulars were on their way, no one knew if casualties had been taken at Lexington, but the word was that shots had probably been fired. Blood continued: "I joined the company under Nathan Barrett at the old court house at about 3 o'clock and was ordered to go into the court house to draw ammunition." This was not a drill. The troops were joined by

minutemen from Lincoln and the group marched to Meriam
Hill. At first light, Blood reported, they "saw the British coming
down Brooks Hill. The sun shined on their arms and they made
a noble appearance in their red coats." It was an intimidating
sight and the colonists turned tail, crossing Old North Bridge,
making for the higher, wild ground of Punkatasset Hill, the
Indian Hill where Robert Blood, a century before, had regularly hunted. They were, Blood remembered, "followed by two
companies of British, one that destroyed some of the stores at
Col. James Barrett's and the other that tarried near the bridge."
The Concord minutemen were essentially cut off from the town
they were supposed to be protecting. "Around 9 o'clock," Thaddeus reported, "we saw a smoke rise at the courthouse." After
discovering a cache of lead bullets, dumping them in a nearby
pond, and digging up three hidden cannons, the British forces
had built a pyre of wooden gun carriages at the center of town
and set it ablaze. The fire had quickly gotten out of control,
however, and threatened to burn down the courthouse.[33]

To the soldiers on Punkatasset Hill, it looked like all of
Concord was being torched. "It was proposed we march into
town," Blood wrote, but the British troops were still stationed at
North Bridge, forbidding their advance. But advance they did,
and the British retreated across the bridge, taking up several of
the planks on their way in an effort to slow the provincial forces
down. According to Blood, James Barrett forbade his men from
firing first on the British troops, but as they approached the
regulars at the banks of the Concord River, these commands
seemed increasingly remote. And it is here, at this decisive moment, where things get interestingly confusing.

Blood wrote that as Barrett's company descended the hill,
with strict orders not to fire on the British, "at that time, an

officer rode up and a gun was fired." This was the shot heard
round the world. "I saw where the Ball threw up the water
about the middle of the river, then a second and third shot, and
the cry FIRE was made from front to rear." The battle was on.
"I think it was not more than two minutes if that much till the
British run and the fire ceased." Victory by Blood's written account. There is, however, a slightly different version of the story,
one that Blood, in the twilight of his life, managed to convey
to Emerson (if not Ripley). Emerson writes out the account in a
notebook dated 1835, although the notebook was undoubtedly
used on many occasions in subsequent years.[34]

"'It could scarcely be called a fight,' Thaddeus Blood said,
'there was no fife or drum that day.'"[35] Women and children
had gathered around the soldiers at the top of the hill overlooking the Old Manse, and some attempt was made by a few of
the men to direct them—and the barking dogs that had joined
the fray—to safety. Thaddeus remembered that the minutemen
were scared, telling Emerson that "Capt Barrett said all sorts
of cheering things to his men" while they looked on as British
regulars chopped down the liberty pole at the center of town.
Cheering things: "Do you think you can fight 'em?"[36] Those
were Barrett's words, according to Blood. The question was
supposed to be rhetorical and energizing, but perhaps it wasn't.
The trees and pastures behind the minutemen led to the safety
of Blood Farm. But when Lieutenant Hosmer pointed to the
smoke billowing up from Concord and asked his fellow men if
they were just going to stand around and "let the town burn,"
the provincial forces pushed down the slope. But these men
hoped they would not have to fire on the grenadiers, some of
whom had taken up firing positions along the riverbank. The
colonists were still, in Blood's words, relayed by Emerson, "the

King's subjects" and "did not want to fight." A warning shot—
fired intentionally or by accident—however, sounded from the
British line and fell harmlessly in the river.[37]

"When they had fired," Blood told Emerson, "there were
several men riding about on horseback. There was Uncle Blood
with his cap and he waved his cap and cried 'fire damn 'em'
and every man shouted fire all along the line, and before the
men could prime their guns again, the British regulars were
running like a flock of sheep."[38] Who was this "Uncle Blood"
who may have sparked the American Revolution? Obviously a
close relation of Thaddeus, otherwise the "uncle" wouldn't have
been appropriate. The heroic figure seems to fit the mold of Maj.
John Buttrick, who helped lead the militia and supposedly entreated his men by yelling, "Fire, fellow soldiers, fire!" Thaddeus
and the major were related by blood, although more distantly
than the word "uncle" might suggest. Emerson, for one, understood Buttrick to be the man who ordered the first shot. Perhaps
the aged Thaddeus was right: "the truth will never be known."
One thing, however, is true—this shot became the irreversible,
irrevocable act that set the Revolutionary War in motion. If the
United States was born at the end of the war in 1781, American
Bloods were present at the very conception.[39]

After the smoke from the Battle of Concord cleared, after
the British retreated to Boston, Thaddeus Blood accompanied
the Concord company to Hull, a small seaside town on the
southern tip of Boston Harbor. In 1776, he was among the provincial troops who captured the British Seventy-First Regiment
of Foot, known as Fraser's Highlanders, headed by Lt. Col. Ar-
chibald Campbell, one of the most significant coups of the war.
Campbell was taken back to the Concord jail (and by some
accounts ridiculed and denied food) but was ultimately traded

as a prisoner of war for the famous Revolutionary frontiersman Ethan Allen.[40] Blood served admirably during the military campaign—and received a pension for his duties—returning to Concord an esteemed figure. Emerson called him "Master Blood" since he spent his later life as one of the town's schoolmasters. Thaddeus the minuteman was involved in Concord town life, but also was happy enough to withdraw into his own quiet corner of Blood Farm. At the age of forty-six, he lost two of his daughters, Hannah and Cynthia, days apart in 1801, to the same disease. He started to donate money to Harvard Divinity School. He grew old relatively peacefully. It had been a full life. By the time Ripley and Emerson came to visit, Blood was spent. Perhaps one early morning of radical self-reliance, one battle that would go down in history, was all one could expect from life or from oneself. Or perhaps Blood was just tired of gilding the lily—embellishing a moment of his life into an iconic moment of freedom.

WHEN RALPH WALDO EMERSON bade Thaddeus Blood goodbye in July 1835, it was with a distinct impression that would color the whole of his philosophy: that courage and true independence are shockingly rare; that individuals sometimes had to be goaded into heroism; that they often teetered on the brink of cowardice; that they are, most likely, already mired in a history and situation that makes bravery next to impossible.

The Concord Bicentennial, scheduled for September 12, 1835, approached with impending speed. Now that he had talked to the last minuteman, Emerson had to get ready. The point to make, if Emerson could express it, was something like the miracle of commonplace courage: the way that heroism can percolate up from the most unlikely places, like phosphorescent gas from a swamp. If Thaddeus Blood could be a hero, anybody could. This wasn't to belittle Blood, not at all (Blood would be Emerson's honored guest at the address). The objective was to even the playing field between Revolutionary heroes and the inhabitants of the present. Freedom fighters were born human and ultimately died that way. The capacity for freedom is nothing special until it is—and then only fleetingly.

In his address, Emerson reports that "in all the anecdotes of that day's events [of the Concord fight] we may discern the natural actions of the people. It was not an extravagant ebullition of feeling, but might have been calculated on by any one acquainted with the spirits and habits of our community."[41] Emerson was cutting pomp and circumstance down to size. He wasn't being cynical but rather realistic, human, and hopeful. Emerson explained that "those poor farmers who came up, that day, to defend their native soil, acted from the simplest instincts. They did not know it was a deed of fame they were doing. They did not babble of glory . . . They [just] supposed they had the right to their corn and their cattle without paying tribute to any but their own governors."[42] Radical freedom and heroism was simply the obvious byproduct of one's natural rights—the sense that a person could not be stripped of their livelihood without consequence, that one's dignity and liberty was more important than immediate safety or security.

The years that followed this address—and his encounter with Blood in 1835—were fortuitous for Emerson and, in hindsight, momentous for American philosophy. It is difficult not to read these productive years as an outgrowth of the meeting between a freedom fighter at the end of life and a young man attempting to renegotiate the possibilities for freedom in the nineteenth century. In the year of his conversation with Blood about the "shot heard round the world," Emerson sat in the second floor of the Old Manse, on the very site of James Blood's onetime home, and wrote the first draft of "Nature," arguably his first and greatest philosophical accomplishment. "Nature" argues, in short, that what is most important is not "what lies behind you or in front of you, [but rather always what] lies inside of you." Plumb the depths—that is Emerson's abiding instruction. The men at the top of Punkatasset Hill overlooking Old North Bridge had little choice but to look inside before they ran back into Concord at the outset of the Revolution. In moments of quiet reflection, recent slaveholders had been forced to search within before fighting for freedom, while inhabiting and protecting a land of bondage. "Always do what you are afraid to do," Emerson regularly echoed his aunt Mary Moody Emerson.[43] Do not turn away. Perhaps Blood managed to face what he was afraid to do in 1776, but the task for his descendants would be to remain resolute in the coming century.

At the end of Thaddeus Blood's account of the Concord fight, he wrote that after the first shots were fired, pandemonium ensued, or something that looked like pandemonium: literally a "free for all." In his words, "after the fire everyone appeared to be his own commander." This was a classic case of "positive liberty": I shall be my own master.[44]

Emerson channeled this minuteman's spirit in "The Concord Address" but also in the lectures that he gave in startlingly quick succession in the second half of the 1830s at the Masonic Temple, which once loomed over the corner of Tremont Street and Temple Place in Boston. While these lectures, delivered in 1836 and 1837, were never published in their original form, they provided the basis of Emerson's philosophy of individualism, nonconformity, and existential responsibility. They were, in many cases, the precursors to his first series of essays, published in 1841, particularly his most famous, "Self-Reliance." Emerson asks his reader to "trust thyself—every heart vibrates to that iron string," and maintains, to the end, that "whoso would be a man, must be a non-conformist." These kernels of Emersonian wisdom, which sought to preserve something of the previous generation's rebellious spirit, were, even at the time, too easily turned into slogans or jingles. But what Emerson was after, what he tried to quicken in the American blood, was a sense that a citizen could—at crucial moments and repeatedly—lay claim to their destiny, be their own commander in a world that was intent on subduing its inhabitants. Emerson writes: "What I must do is all that concerns me, not what the people think. This rule . . . may serve for the whole distinction between greatness and meanness . . . It is easy in the world to live after the world's opinion; it is easy in solitude to live after our own; but the great man is he who in the midst of the crowd keeps with perfect sweetness the independence of solitude." Emerson was concerned—and it was not an empty worry—that independence was not a matter of making a onetime declaration, that a single battle was not nearly enough to secure human dignity, that preserving political autonomy in the name of individual liberty was only one aspect, albeit an important one, of meaningful revolution. Establishing institutions based on equality, justice, and freedom: that was the ongoing and forward-looking object of revolutionary activity.

"The American Scholar," a speech that Emerson delivered at the invitation of the Phi Beta Kappa Society in Cambridge on August 31, 1837, and which Oliver Wendell Holmes called the nation's "intellectual declaration of independence," was given as an imperative to think originally, but also to act boldly in a world that simultaneously beckons and threatens:

> The world,—this shadow of the soul, or *other me*, lies wide around. Its attractions are the keys which unlock my thoughts and make me acquainted with myself. I run eagerly into this resounding tumult. I grasp the hands of those next to me, and take my place in the ring to suffer and to work, taught by an instinct that so shall the dumb abyss be vocal with speech. I pierce its order; I dissipate its fear; I dispose of it within the circuit of my expanding life. So much only of life as I know by experience, so much of the wilderness have I vanquished and planted, or so far have I extended my being, my dominion. I do not see how any man can afford, for the sake of his nerves and his nap, to spare any action in which he can partake.[45]

Emerson was hitting his transcendentalist stride, in the footsteps of Romantic authors like Samuel Coleridge and Johann Wolfgang von Goethe, but also in a path cut by common men or men of the world, like Thaddeus Blood, who had not, at least according to national mythology, shirked his duties in succumbing to anxiety or exhaustion. The large audience at the Phi Beta Kappa address roared their applause.

"The American Scholar" had been an opening salvo, but something more decisive had to be performed if Emerson was to prove that he was willing to "run eagerly into this resounding tumult." He drafted "The Divinity School Address," delivered before the senior class in Harvard's Divinity College on Sunday evening, July 15, 1838: almost three years, to the day, after his visit to interview Thaddeus Blood. The memory of the old man seems to haunt the address, which proved to be Emerson's "shot heard round the world": "Wherever a man comes, there comes revolution." Emerson continues, explaining, "Man is the wonderworker. He is seen amid miracles."[46] On this night, Emerson attacked, relentlessly, the ways of Old World religion that continued to hold sway in the staid intellectual community of Harvard. God was not enshrined in good books or doctrines or severe preachers but in the lives of average people who occasionally proved that improbable miracles were still completely possible. The battle lines between Emerson's budding transcendentalism and the well-entrenched legacy of Puritanism that continued to dominate New England after the Revolution, the battle lines between the promise of America and the stultifying practices of the past, were once again drawn. This conflict lasted a long time: Emerson was banned from speaking on Harvard's campus for three decades. He ultimately prevailed (who remembers the countless thinkers who opposed Emerson in the 1840s?), but at the time it would be a brutal intellectual fight.

In 1841, six years after his meeting with Thaddeus, Emerson was still thinking about the words of the American Blood. In a journal from that year, Emerson recalls that "Blood's impression plainly was that there was no great courage exhibited but from a few . . . I suppose we know how brave they were by considering how the present inhabitants would behave in like emergency."[47] The men and women of Concord in 1775 were still just men and women, and acted as weakly or heroically as anyone else who might be placed in similar circumstances. In 1841, Emerson concludes his personal reflection on Blood: "It is plain that there is little of that two-o'clock-in-the-morning-type-of-courage, which Napoleon said he had known few to possess." Thaddeus Blood had a measure of it, and Emerson hoped that Blood was not alone. Emerson's intent in the Concord Bicentennial address, in his philosophy on the whole, was to focus his audience's attention on the chance to be his or her "own commander." A person must act while they still have the opportunity.

Thaddeus Blood died at the age of eighty-nine in 1844. By then, his onetime interlocutor, Emerson, had crossed into middle age, having made a name for himself as the "sage of Concord" and the poet of freedom. Thaddeus served as schoolmaster in Concord, and was known about town as "Master Blood," but the aged educator was most likely unequipped to grasp the philosophical significance and political implication of Emerson's writings. Nonetheless, Blood's casting of positive liberty in the Revolution—a force that occasionally emerged in the course of everyday life—had helped Emerson to democratize heroism, to recognize the hidden grandeur in average farmers like the Bloods. Thaddeus may have also inspired Emerson to undertake his own form of revolt against the intellectual and spiritual traditions that held sway over Harvard and, by extension, nineteenth-century New England. These were Emerson's acts of insurrection in the 1830s and 1840s, embodied in lectures and essays that would ignite American transcendentalism. This form of rebellion, however, was largely intellectual. It was not necessarily something that the minutemen on Punkatasset Hill could have easily understood. Even Master Blood, despite his education and commitment to schooling, might have found Emerson's poetry and sermons a bit esoteric. Indeed, some of Emerson's closest friends—like Margaret Fuller (who was more than capable of following him intellectually)—thought the sage needed to tether his concerns a bit more firmly to the ground of human relations. There were revolutions—*real* ones—to be fought in *this* world. Thaddeus Blood died at the moment Emerson came alive to face the great battle of his own age. It was one that Thaddeus, as a child, could have scarcely imagined. It was, however, firmly rooted at Blood Farm.

IN THE YEAR that Thaddeus Blood died, Emerson delivered "On the Emancipation of Negroes in the British West Indies" to an audience at the Concord courthouse. It was his first of many antislavery addresses. This was not the abolitionists' "shot heard round the world"; Emerson's mentor William Ellery Channing, known as the "apostle of Unitarianism," had been protesting slavery for seven years before Emerson rallied his inner troops. But now the apostle of transcendentalism cast his lot with the abolitionists, led by his contemporaries William Lloyd Garrison and Lydia Maria Child. The lecture was organized by thirteen Massachusetts towns to celebrate the tenth anniversary of the emancipation of African slaves in the Indies, and Emerson had been invited to give the address. The doors of most buildings in Concord were open to Emerson at this point in his life, but for this controversial lecture, not a single venue was available.[48] The residents of Concord were, once again, unprepared to make sacrifices for freedom. Eventually, the courthouse was secured by the wiles of one of Emerson's friends, a twenty-seven-year-old wild child by the name of Henry David Thoreau. At the lecture's appointed time, Thoreau rang the town bell to welcome, to alert, to warn his neighbors.[49] And many of them came, whether intentionally or accidentally, to confront the excruciating reality that Emerson highlighted, if not revealed:

I am heart-sick when I read how [the slaves] came [to the Indies], and how they are kept there. Their case was left out of the mind and out of the heart of their brothers. The prizes of society, the trumpet of fame, the privileges of learning, of culture, of religion, the decencies and joys of marriage, honor, obedience, personal authority, and a perpetual melioration into a finer civility, these were for all, but not for them. For the negro, was the slave-ship to begin with, in whose filthy hold he sat in irons, unable to lie down; bad food, and insufficiency of that; disfranchisement; no property in the rags that covered him; no marriage, no right in the poor black woman that cherished him in her bosom,—no right to the children of his body; no security from the humors, none from the crimes, none from the appetites of his master: toil, famine, insult, and flogging; and, when he sunk in the furrow, no wind of good fame blew over him, no priest of salvation visited him with glad tidings: but he went down to death, with dusky dreams of African shadow-catchers and Obeahs hunting him.[50]

This was probably only slightly more brutal than the story of Frank, the enslaved Black man who lived and worked at William Emerson's Old Manse, or of Dinah or Thomas Farwell, who spent most of their lives on Blood Farm. However, what Emerson describes is certainly no worse than Robert Blood of Groton allowing his enslaved boy to be poisoned. Of course, Emerson, and certainly Thoreau, knew that the residents of Concord and the surrounding communities were now, as ever, culpable for their comfortable ways of life, complicit in a moral disaster of slavery and class inequality. Of course, there was more than enough blame to go around. But Emerson believed, in 1844, that the time was ripe to act. To work against, if not to rectify, this history.

By that point, William Grimes had published his grueling firsthand account of slavery in a country that was completely underpinned by the institution. "If it were not for the stripes on my back which were made while I was a slave," Grimes wrote in 1825, "I would in my will, leave my skin a legacy to the government, desiring that it might be taken off and made into parchment, and then bind the constitution of glorious happy and free America."[51] Following Grimes (yet in a more tepid fashion), Emerson maintained that the "enterprise" of the United States, the "very muscular vigor of this nation, is inconsistent with slavery."[52] I've often wondered whether this is true in any precise way, but Emerson's conclusion is so hopeful that it is hard to find fault: "The Intellect, with blazing eye, looking through history from the beginning onward, gazes on this blot, and it disappears. The sentiment of Right, once very low and indistinct, but ever more articulate, because it is the voice of the universe, pronounces Freedom."[53]

Emerson and Thoreau spent the better part of the next two decades walking together across North Bridge, up Punkatasset Hill, through Estabrook Woods to Mason's Pasture. They'd often make their way north through Blood Farm discussing the nature of freedom, its limits, and, increasingly, the injustice of bondage.

Thaddeus Blood was gone. He might not have understood anyway. A new sort of revolution was upon them. Thoreau was a zealot for justice, one who believed so fervently in the sanctity and universality of the human spirit that most forms of society seemed wholly stifling. The woods and swamps surrounding Concord were his sanctuary, the place where he would go for perspective on a world that threatened to implode at any moment. He took an aging Emerson with him, away from the manse, once owned by James Blood, through the wilds once occupied by John and Robert Blood.

Sometimes, Emerson and Thoreau would go at night—the darker the better. Thoreau had made a dear friend in the woods next to Tophet Swamp: an old man who sat in his nightshirt, in the shadows, in his woodshed, in a swivel chair. With a telescope. Freedom would mean pitifully little if one couldn't gaze up at the night sky, distant yet beckoning. This strange and bewitching man was none other than the hermit son of Thaddeus Blood.

THE STARGAZER ≡

The story of Romulus and Remus being suckled
by a wolf is not a meaningless fable.

—HENRY DAVID THOREAU,
JOURNAL, FEBRUARY 1851[1]

IF THADDEUS BLOOD REPRESENTED LIBERTY IN ITS
historical and political manifestations—and its epic transformative power—his son, Perez, exemplified the flip side of American
independence. Perez embodied what Isaiah Berlin called "negative liberty," a radical freedom from constraint or interference
by others. Perez lived in the northernmost corner of Estabrook
Woods, on the edge of Concord, in the deeper, increasingly
barren region of Blood Farm. Born in the summer of 1785,
Perez was raised in a time of founders, formers, and joiners—
individuals who spent their lives constructing, and participat-
ing in, the more perfect union that was to become the United
States. His father was surely one of them. As an adult in the
1830s, Perez witnessed the birth of the Industrial Revolution,
the expansion of the railroad, and the construction of large
cotton mills, such as those that sprang up in Lowell, Massachu-

setts, seven miles north of Blood Farm. Perez hunkered down in the Estabrook Woods and watched many of his neighbors and relatives choose a different path. They left their farming communities, moving to urban centers in the East or journeying to the fertile and lucrative lands of the American West. In both cases, travelers typically moved en masse, forming communities that would reflect at least the semblance of civilization. This migration, however, had another effect on the Estabrook: hay fields quickly reverted to wilderness.

The land of Blood Farm had been cleared for hundreds of years, first by the Native Americans in controlled burns, and then by generations of Blood farmers. During Perez's lifetime, however, these once plowed meadows grew into untended pasture, which morphed with surprising speed into bushland and fledgling forest. Abandoned farmhouses collapsed under their own weight; walls crumbled; roads were abandoned and immediately overgrown. When one walked through the Estabrook, sometimes the only sign of human occupation was the occasional cellar hole, but even this was typically the site of not-so-new vegetation. This was the world of Perez Blood.

Perez's human neighbors to the north and west—the Greens, Masons, and Minots—still ran sustainable family farms at the edges of the Estabrook. Indeed, the land around Concord, for the most part, teemed with human activity through the 1840s, even as the majority of Blood Farm returned to its primitive state. Industrious farmers grew diverse crops—from asparagus to beans to melons—that supported their families and the surrounding community, actively managed their fields, built new walls to cordon off the land, and drove their cattle north to high pastures and then south to Boston to be butchered. The forests of white pine that surrounded Billerica and Concord were ideal for making pails, baskets, and barrels (how else was one to store and transport the largesse of modern life?), and harder wood, primarily oak, was harvested at increasing rates.

Perez's land, however, was different. It was decidedly out of the way. Perez's tract of the Estabrook was connected to Concord by Two Rod Road, although the once wide and accommodating road had been reduced to a narrow bridle path. When a person died in the wilderness of the Estabrook, family members had to carry the corpse to the burial grounds at Concord. On the path remain two "mort stones," flat slabs of granite approximately five feet long. The mort stones were way-points on a long and difficult trek, a place where a corpse could be set down for a moment on its final journey to town. These stones—often regarded as haunted or cursed—were signs of the relative remoteness of Blood's home.[2] Only truly desolate roads required mort stones.

The forests immediately surrounding Perez's house continued to grow. He owned a sizable woodlot that was never cleared. He lived with his two unmarried sisters, Polly and Cynthia, in the house of his minuteman father, Thaddeus, in an ancient grove of oak trees that for decades remained untouched by any saw.[3] A boulder field stretched south from the house to Punkatasset Hill, where the transcendentalist poet William Ellery Channing (not to be confused for his antislavery uncle William) kept a small cottage. Channing described the Blood territory in his "The Barren Moors":

> On your bare rocks, O barren moors,
> On your bare rocks I love to lie!—
> They stand like crags upon the shores,
> Or clouds upon a placid sky . . .

A serious place distinct from all
Which busy Life delights to feel,—
I stand in this deserted hall,
And thus the wounds of time conceal.[4]

The home of Perez was no place for the delights—or trivialities—of the "busy Life." It was the most foreboding and deserted of places.

Perez's isolation was not a function of poverty but seems to have been premeditated and chosen freely. He was supposedly college educated, although Harvard has no account of a student named Perez, or the more common Peter, Blood. The founding document of the Concord Lyceum, however, which has been described as "one of the largest, strongest, and longest-lived of all the lyceums" of nineteenth-century America, mentions him as one of the founding members.[5] The lyceum was a New England intellectual establishment, a place where the best and brightest scholars of the nineteenth century gave public lectures to surprisingly large audiences. Founded in 1829, it was where the Concord transcendentalists, like Emerson and Thoreau, cut their oratorical teeth. That Perez Blood was present at the creation of this institution suggests that his life in the forest outside town was not altogether typical: he was a cultivated man who willingly lived in uncultivated hinterlands.

When his father died in 1844, Perez inherited a small sum of money. The prudent thing to do with the inheritance would have been to invest in new farm equipment, to hire a hand to tend the garden, to fill his woodshed, or simply to move out of the woods. This is undoubtedly what his practically minded neighbors, enthralled with the "busy Life," would have done. Perez had other ideas. Perhaps there is wisdom in acting imprudently, in slowing things down against the grain. He fashioned an observatory with a swivel chair that could be raised and lowered as needed. Then he spent his inheritance on a telescope and a celestial globe. Galileo had used a thirty-two-power scope with which he founded modern astronomy.[6] The bachelor of Estabrook Woods had an instrument more than twice as powerful. By some accounts, he only bought the materials for the telescope, and built it himself. Perez had inherited his father's interest in freedom but also in divinity (whether he continued to donate to Harvard Divinity after Thaddeus's death is unknown). In any event, Perez knew that it is probably a mistake, a grievous one, to confuse the immediate, mundane concerns of life with far-reaching questions of existence. Enlightenment,

Henry David
Thoreau

Emerson reminds his readers, cannot be realized by mimicry or the study of history but only in the individual exploration of nature. Perez searched the skies, largely by himself—a reclusive, eccentric man who only occasionally greeted fellow outsiders. There was a certain freedom in being eccentric—in being slightly "out of center," in maintaining a slightly or wholly different orbit.

On September 6, 1847, Henry David Thoreau ended his famous two-year experiment at Walden Pond, located three miles to the south of Blood Farm. Thoreau's time at Walden had been a brief respite from the cultural bustle of life in Concord's center. The signs of modern industry were all around him—the new railway was a short walk from his hut that had been purchased from an Irish worker who helped install the tracks—but Thoreau's attempt to "live deliberately, to front only the essential facts of life" was at once the attempt to live apart from the conventions of American society that seemed increasingly out of sync with the basic pulse of human existence. "Simplify, Simplify!" was Thoreau's command.[7] According to Thoreau, there were plenty of simpletons in Concord Center— oafish fools who spent (or wasted) their lives on amassing larger farms and bank accounts, behavior that was clearly at odds with Thoreauvian simplicity. Citizens could dutifully play their roles in the maintenance of a nation and the entrenchment of capitalism, and they often did so in the name of freedom, maintaining that they were most free when they participated in the expansion of American independence through individual conspicuous consumption. Thoreau, however, routinely protested the grand narrative of liberal democracy and suspected that what most of his fellow citizens called "the free life" was actually a form of self-imposed bondage, and, even worse, that the freedom of the majority of wealthy citizens was premised on the subjection of countless others.

In 1846, Thoreau's protest of the American establishment took a turn that many an American Blood would have appreciated: he stopped paying his taxes. For Thoreau, it wasn't enough for the state to fulfill its basic social contract: a government had to act in such a way—politically, but also morally—to earn the loyalty of its citizens. When the Mexican-American War broke out that year, many Northerners, Thoreau included, understood it as an attempt to expand the institution of slavery in the United States. Such a state would not receive his financial support. There were, however, consequences to resisting authority: on July 23, 1846, Sam Staples, Concord's constable-cum–tax collector, escorted Thoreau to the Concord jail, where he spent the night. He would have remained there if an unnamed friend—perhaps Emerson—had not paid the fine and the back taxes.[8]

The fall of 1847 was a pivotal season for Thoreau. He was thirty, and though he'd been jailed, albeit briefly, for the sake of his conscience, he had relatively little to show for his conviction. He had yet to write a book of any substance and his reputation as a lecturer was far from secure. The question loomed: Would Henry David Thoreau abandon his youthful experiments and grow up? Upon leaving Walden, he was, in his words, "a sojourner in civilized life again."[9] His friendship with Emerson had deepened in the previous year. At least that was something essential to pursue. Emerson was scheduled to lecture in England in the fall of 1847, and Lidian Emerson, his wife, invited Thoreau to board with the family in Emerson's absence, but before he left for Europe, Emerson joined Thoreau on a final autumn perambulation of the hills behind Concord. It was the path that Emerson had followed with Ezra Ripley more than a decade earlier.[10] But this time, with Thoreau as his companion, he set out in near darkness on a clear night, walking north along Two Rod Road toward a now familiar house nestled in a stand of ancient oaks. Behind the house was a woodshed, and in the woodshed, the two philosophers found their old friend Perez Blood, a man whose uncanny life has been preserved almost exclusively in the writings of his two philosopher-admirers.

"He had not gone to bed," Thoreau wrote of Perez to his sister Sophia, "but was sitting in the woodshed, in the dark, alone, in his astronomical chair, which is all legs and rounds, with a seat which can be inserted at any height."[11] Woodsheds are supposed to be filled to the roof in the fall, packed with fuel to see a large family through the winter. Blood lived only with his two sisters, and seemed wholly uninterested in the practical concern of impending cold. Perez's woodshed was his observation deck. The responsibilities of chopping and stacking wood were forgone for the otherworldly freedom of stargazing. To staid Concordians, Perez's actions would have been truly wild, but wildness was, at least in part, what drew Thoreau and Emerson to Blood Farm in the summer of 1847. It is possible that this was not the first trip to see Perez, either. In the first detailed entry regarding Thoreau, in 1838, Emerson describes a walk near the Estabrook and makes a remark that could seem a non sequitur: "We [meaning Emerson and Thoreau] agreed that the seeing of the stars through a telescope would be worth all the astronomical lectures." The only telescope in Estabrook Woods was owned by Perez Blood.

In the basement of the Concord Public Library, stowed safely in the "vault," are three boxes of papers from Emerson's library. One of them contains the notes dated July 30, 1835, from Emerson's interview of Thaddeus Blood in preparation for the minutemen obelisk dedication. In the same box, undated, unlabeled, seemingly untouched, is a strange yet beautiful fragment, written in the loose hand of a slightly older Emerson:

> The lantern which the astronomer used to find his objects and glasses seemed to disturb him and hinder him from seeing the heavens, and though it was turned down lower and lower he was still impatient and could not see till it was fully put out. When it was gone and I had accustomed myself to the telescope the little garret grew positively lightsome, and the lantern would have been annoying to all of us. The astronomer was calm and kind and surveyed the sky to find the most renowned points, and unlike any other showman, relieved of all responsibility, since Nature was at the expense of the entertainment. I saw the dumbbell nebula in the fox and goose constellation and . . . what was reckoned to be the farthest reaches of Nature, the nebula of Orion. We were well entertained and apprehended once again the vastness of nature—how enormous the lesson is we have to learn.[12]

Was this Perez? It could scarcely be otherwise. If Blood impressed Emerson, he utterly captivated Thoreau, who wrote, "We saw Saturn's rings, and the mountains in the moon, and the shadows in their craters, and the sunlight on the spurs of the mountains in the dark portion."[13] Saturn and the moon were the astrological signs of age and youth. Saturn—old Father Time—insists that one check the watch, be punctual and mindful to the end. The moon gives no such instruction, drawing young spirits into the night where time stands still or disappears without notice. Saturn or the moon: this is the choice that Thoreau and Emerson, that all of us, have to make in life. To what extent must we grow up? Saturn tracks its planetary cycle with near perfect regularity. Every thirty years, give or take a few, it comes full circle, just as individuals cycle through early adulthood and middle age. In 1847, Thoreau was thirty, Saturn was back, and Perez Blood stood at the meeting place. None of this is to insist in no uncertain terms that Thoreau was driven by astrological forces or that Perez Blood's presence in Thoreau's life had mystical significance. I am, however, no longer willing to fully ignore the wild possibility. It is quite clear that Thoreau's friendship with Perez was lasting and profound (at least for Henry), and this turns out to be fascinating enough.

Thoreau could see his future self in Blood: an educated man, unmarried but tethered to his family of origin, a man who would defy the expectations of his practically minded neighbors, retreat to the wilderness, and spend his last years in the contemplation and careful observation of nature. After his night in Perez's woodshed, Thoreau accompanied the old man to the newly outfitted observatory at Harvard to look through the telescope of Professor Benjamin Peirce (the notoriously gruff father of Charles Sanders Peirce). Thoreau wrote to Emerson on November 14, 1847, that "Mr. [Perez] Blood and his company have at length seen the stars through the great telescope, and he told me that he thought it was worth the while. Mr. [Benjamin] Peirce made him wait till the crowd had dispersed (it was a Saturday evening), and then was quite polite,—conversed with him, and showed him the micrometer, etc.; and he said Mr. Blood's glass was large enough for all ordinary astronomical work."[14]

While visiting Harvard, Thoreau and Blood discussed with Peirce the hotly contested discovery of Neptune, which had been made the previous year and with which Peirce was intimately involved. Neptune was the first planet to be discovered by mathematics and prediction rather than by simple observation. Peirce had some serious misgivings about the calculations that had been used by Urbain Le Verrier, the French discoverer of the planet, but the emergence of Neptune signaled a turn in the study of the skies. No longer was it enough to simply observe and chart the heavens. The universe operated by mechanical laws and was therefore, at least in theory, predictable. Perez was impressed by, and grateful for, Peirce's demonstration and discussion, but confessed to Thoreau "that he [was] too old to study the calculus or higher mathematics"[15] that would allow for such prediction and discoveries. Blood would content himself with the view from his wild promontory outside Concord. Thoreau seemed to be of a similar mind, sanguine regarding the possibilities of modern science, while wary of the way it stood to reduce the natural world to a discrete number of calculable forces. Thoreau believed that nature—which included human nature—remained happily irreducible. It would neither be exhaustively explained by science nor completely hemmed in by the boundaries of civilized life. All of nature was essentially eccentric.

In the months subsequent to his first encounter with Blood, Thoreau began to formulate a lecture titled "The Rights and Duties of the Individual in Relation to Government," delivered in February 1848, which would later be published as "Civil Disobedience," arguably Thoreau's most famous essay. A treatise framed by the injustices of slavery, it is a call for men and women of conscience to resist any government that would permit such an institution to arise. "I cannot for an instant," Thoreau wrote, "recognize that political organization as my

government which is the slave's government also."[16] "Civil Disobedience" is also a biting criticism of the habits of modern
American life, the way that they tend to level out individuality
and particularity. Most of Thoreau's exposure to this habitual
mode of life was through his now daily walks into the Estabrook
and to the small towns that surrounded Concord. The neighbors he encountered, quite frankly, disgusted him:

> The mass of men serve the state thus, not as men mainly,
> but as machines, with their bodies. They are the standing
> army, and the militia, jailers, constables, posse comitatus,
> etc. In most cases there is no free exercise whatever of the
> judgment or of the moral sense; but they put themselves on
> a level with wood and earth and stones; and wooden men
> can perhaps be manufactured that will serve the purpose
> as well. Such command no more respect than men of straw
> or a lump of dirt. They have the same sort of worth only
> as horses and dogs. Yet such as these even are commonly
> esteemed good citizens.[17]

Thoreau was aware that those individuals who exercise free
judgment and moral sense, who take the liberty to go against
the grain of convention, are often regarded as lesser citizens,
as misfits and renegades. Thoreau, out of principle as much as
curiosity, was repeatedly attracted to such individuals. Indeed,
after leaving Walden, the original site of his civil resistance, he
slowly became even more of an outlier, and Perez Blood certainly would have been an inspiration.

In the late 1840s, Estabrook Woods, Blood's backyard, became Thoreau's favorite place to saunter. He would write in
the morning—often in his monumental journal—and walk in the

afternoon. In the fall of 1851, he was hired to put his walking to work; he was employed as the surveyor tasked with defining the border between Concord and Carlisle, directly across from Blood's property. At the time, the border between the sister towns had a dozen stark angles, rock walls that parceled out land fiercely contested in the time of Robert Blood. In fact, it was Perez Blood who had preceded Thoreau in the role as town surveyor, and Thoreau routinely mentioned that Blood's measurements were just as, if not more, precise than his own.

Thoreau's job was to smooth and justify the remaining angles of the boundary, to make the border straight, or at least well-marked. At first, he despised his new job. The idea of satisfying some town ordinance by randomly cutting the land in two irked a man who had always regarded Estabrook Woods as inherently untamable. Walking across property lines brought him into contact with the few inhabitants who remained on Blood Farm, and this was, for Thoreau, one of the more difficult parts of the task. It wasn't that Thoreau hated the average Carlisle farmer, but that he worried about becoming one himself. There was something soul-deadening about this prospect, which for Thoreau was worse than a man succumbing to vice. Isaiah Green, Perez's only immediate neighbor in the 1850s, who lived a quarter mile from Blood, was one of the men Thoreau encountered and regarded with equal parts pity and disdain, writing:

> The retirement in which Green has lived for nearly eighty years in Carlisle is a retirement very different from and much greater than that in which the pioneer dwells at the west, for the latter dwells within the sound and the surf of those billows of migration which are breaking on the shores around him or near him of the west—but those billows have

long since swept over the spot which Green inhabits and left him in the calm sea—There is something exceedingly pathetic to think of in which a life as he must have lived—of no more to redeem it—such a life as an average Carlisle man may supposed to have drawn out to eighty years.[18]

Thoreau wrote in his journal that a man like Green died and "has nothing but the mark of his cider mill left. Here was the cider mill and there the orchard and there the hay pasture— and so men lived and drank and passed away . . . That is the life of these select-men! Spun out. They will be forgotten in a few years even by such as themselves like vermin."[19]

Vermin: pests, parasites, vectors of disease, which spread with stunning speed. How to inoculate American culture against the forces of materialism, habit, and banality? Thoreau's answer was not a standard one. Retreating from the Estabrook, leaving men like Green behind, would have been the easiest course of action. Given his education, one might expect Thoreau to have lived a more cosmopolitan or cultured existence in Boston or New York. Indeed, he occasionally tried. He was, however, unhappy in more sophisticated climes. There was something false, escapist, in this approach. The task of life was to grow up in the Estabrook—a country ever only half-domesticated—and to strive after inspiring, even celestial, ideals. Thoreau concludes his meditation on Isaiah Green with a question: "What would then redeem such a life?" He writes, in a rare moment of hope:

If I could know that there was ever entertained over their cellar hole [in the Estabrook] some divine thought which came as a messenger of the gods—that he who resided here

acted once in his life from a noble impulse—rising superior
to his groveling and penurious life—if only a single verse of
poetry or poetic prose had ever been written or spoken or
conceived here beyond doubt—I should not think it vain
that man had lived here.—It would to some extent be true
that God had lived here.[20]

As it turns out, there was such a man, one who could restore
Thoreau's tenuous faith in humanity, who lived in the wilds
but who acted—at least once in his life and probably many
times—from a noble impulse. Thoreau just needed a proper
reintroduction.

PEREZ BLOOD WAS a fixture in Thoreau's mind, an elderly
man he would have visited regularly on his daily sauntering
routes through the Estabrook. Like many such fixtures, Blood
occasionally goes without explicit mention in Thoreau's journals, temporarily fading from view between the years 1848 and
1851. Blood reemerges, however, in the year of Thoreau's employment as the town surveyor, and this interaction proved decisive for Thoreau, who was, at that very moment, on the brink
of becoming an American literary icon. It is no exaggeration
to suggest that Blood helped Thoreau define his conception of
human freedom—one more unruly and disobedient than Emerson could have ever imagined—in the fall of 1851.

In July, in the midst of the boundary survey, Thoreau
remarks:

I have been to-night with Anthony Wright to look through
Perez Blood's telescope a second time. A dozen of Blood's

neighbors were swept along in the stream of our curiosity. One who lived half a mile this side said that Blood had been down that way within a day or two with his terrestrial, or day, glass, looking into the eastern horizon [at] the hills of Billerica, Burlington, and Woburn. I was amused to see what sort of respect this man with a telescope had obtained from his neighbors, something akin to that which savages award to civilized men though in this case the interval between the parties was very slight.[21]

On the same night, Thoreau reflects that Blood "with his skull-cap on, his short figure, his north European figure, made me think of Tycho Brahe. He did not invite us into his house this cool evening—men nor women—nor did he ever before to my knowledge."[22] The comparison between Blood and Brahe, the sixteenth-century Danish nobleman who founded modern astronomy, was apt: both men came from royal families of a kind, chose to be isolated, and spent their days taking careful account of nature. Brahe lived in a secluded castle-observatory, on the island of Hven, in an icy strait between Denmark and Sweden, and built Stjerneborg, a separate "star castle" (a much grander version of Blood's woodshed observation deck), on the outskirt of the estate. Brahe was also the last of the "naked-eye astronomers," who viewed the heavens without the aid of additional technical instruments. He was, first and foremost, a meticulous observer and connoisseur of the night skies. Like Blood, he regularly dwelled in the night air and seemed to believe that life was made of all that one chose not to ignore. Brahe's voluminous catalogs of the heavens indicated that he was forever attentive. He was no Kepler—his scientific rival and mathematical superior—but in an important sense Brahe always maintained the edge. Unlike the nearsighted Kepler, he could actually *see* the stars. Indeed, without Brahe's observations, Kepler wouldn't have had data to analyze. Upon making the comparison between Brahe and Blood in 1851, Thoreau noted, "I am still contented to see the stars with my naked eye."[23]

Thoreau's companion on his visit to Blood was Anthony Wright, a local farmer and lumber merchant. Wright's perspective was a study in contrast with Blood's. He could give an assessment of every woodlot and land parcel in the area—a detailed monetary assessment. Thoreau admired his expertise (Wright was the first to inform Thoreau of the great white oaks in Inches Woods near Sudbury, Massachusetts), but also quietly disdained Wright for interpreting the natural world through the tightly circumscribed lens of profit and cost.[24] When Wright and Thoreau visited Perez, Wright could scarcely believe that an inhabitant of the Estabrook would be interested in the heavens, much less spend his family fortune on an instrument to investigate them. "Mr. Wright," Thoreau wrote, "asked how much [Blood's] instrument cost. [Blood] answered, 'Well, that is something I don't like to tell . . . however I think it is a very proper question.' 'Yes,' said I, 'and I think you have given a very proper answer."[25] Thoreau was relieved to find that Blood had a firm grip on this most basic, but occasionally elusive, reality.

Perez Blood was not particularly well-kept: usually disheveled in a tattered frock coat. Nor was his house grand. But his life radically departed from that of the average woodcutter and farmer who inhabited the Estabrook. In the days that followed their July meeting, Blood asked Thoreau to travel to Cambridge, this time alone, to retrieve astronomical books from

Harvard. The librarian asked Thoreau whom these books were for, obviously impressed by the sophistication and scope of the texts, and bade Thoreau goodbye with the comment that anyone who was able to read such books was welcome to have them. Blood had a unique talent, one that Thoreau deeply admired and emulated: to live simply yet think deeply. Blood's was not the simplicity of a common farmer. Thoreau drew the distinction starkly:

> The savage lives simply through ignorance and idleness or laziness, but the philosopher lives simply through wisdom. In the case of the savage, the accompaniment of simplicity is idleness with its attendant vices, but in the case of the philosopher, it is the highest employment and development . . . the question is whether you can bear freedom.[26]

Blood bore his freedom well. He didn't have to study astronomical charts, or read books, or sit in his woodshed with a telescope. He could have filled his free time at the Black Mansion Tavern, or the Revolutionary Tavern, or the Red Lion— local watering holes where many of his neighbors got besotted on a regular basis. The Black Mansion Tavern, which Thoreau described as the haunt of drinking men from Concord and Bedford, was still in the Blood family. Perez could have easily gotten drunk, gone to sleep, or passed out. But Thoreau's account of the old man indicates that Blood remained wide-eyed and awake to the very end of his days.

As one grows older, there is a tendency, according to Thoreau, to narrow one's angle of vision. Adulthood has the unfortunate consequence of leaving youthful urges and openness

behind. Referencing his interactions with Blood and the dwell-
ers of the Estabrook, Thoreau wrote that "the youth gets together his materials to build a bridge to the moon . . . and at
length the middle aged man concludes to build a woodshed
with them."[27] Of course, it doesn't have to happen this way.
Upon meeting Blood, Thoreau knew that one's woodshed
could be a site of a bridge to the moon, that it was possible to
hold on to the remnants of youth at the age of sixty-five. The
choice between the moon and Saturn, between renewal and
decline, remained just that—a choice. However, as he became
reacquainted with Blood, Thoreau struggled with this decision.
The difficulty was only deepened by an event that took place
along old Carlisle Road, at the entrance to the Estabrook, a few
hundred meters from Perez's house.

In the fall of 1849, James Clark, a landowner on the western edge of the Estabrook, purchased the cabin that Thoreau
had constructed at Walden Pond.[28] This had been Thoreau's
conduit to the moon, a temple or monument to human renewal.
But Clark did what any good farmer would do—he moved the
cabin to his farm and put it to use—as a woodshed. Even the
most wild and idealistic of notions could be repurposed and
tamed.

On a cold December day in 1851, Thoreau was working
on his final manuscript, *Wild Fruits*, a subtle defense of undomesticated natures. On this day, he wrote in his journal: "Saw
Perez Blood in his frock—a stuttering, sure, unpretending man,
who does not speak without thinking, does not guess. When I
reflect on how different he was from his neighbors, Conant,
Mason, Hodgman, I saw that it was not so much outwardly, but
that I saw an inner form."[29] There was something remarkable,
even otherworldly, about Perez Blood. He was the original wild

apple (Thoreau's long-standing emblem): rare, hidden, free to grow as it pleased. Thoreau continued, describing Perez:

> We do, indeed, see through and through each other, through the veil of the body, and see the real form and character in spite of the garment. Any coarseness or tenderness is seen and felt under whatever garb. How nakedly men appear to us! For the spiritual assists the natural eye.[30]

Today, it is tempting to reduce Thoreau's remark to a platitude: outward appearances don't matter; what matters is on the inside. But in the 1850s, as the abolitionist movement mounted in New England and economic inequalities in the United States deepened, Thoreau's comment went to the heart of the nation's moral crisis. What clothing—or skin—one wore was irrelevant to the question of character or, for that matter, freedom. This is one of many interactions that Thoreau would have with the proverbial "nobodies" who occupied the wilderness surrounding his native Concord, but his friendship with Blood was among the most long-standing and meaningful.

Thoreau knew that individuals facing systemic disadvantage went, generally speaking, unnoticed by people of privilege. This is the paradox of political erasure: those who are trammeled in the dealings of a nation rarely get a say in its future. These voices—like Blood's—got lost in the Estabrook. Social justice was in no small part a matter of counteracting myopia, of recognizing the lives of others hidden in plain sight.

In November 1850, Thoreau had an interaction with a Native woman that coincides with his admiration of Blood. Thoreau wrote in his journal: "A squaw came to our house today . . . and said, 'Me want pie.' Theirs is not common begging. You are merely a rich Indian who shares his goods with the poor. They merely offer you the opportunity to be generous and hospitable."[31] Thoreau understood that what kept the rich from understanding the plight of the poor was, in part, the fact of their wealth: not just metaphorically or conceptually, but literally. It's hard to understand the inner lives of others if one is always attending to one's household or rushing off to harvest a woodlot. To "live deliberately," in Thoreau's words, was to wrest oneself from the diversions of modern life, to understand the difference between the supposedly urgent matters of spending and acquiring—what the lumberman Anthony Wright was transfixed by—and the truly significant issues of observing, caring, and thinking. "Do not trouble yourself much to get new things," Thoreau instructs us. "Sell your clothes and keep your thoughts."[32] To be free from the tawdry distractions of modern life—of the endlessly diverting display of the things—allowed a person to focus and think. What could we think, Thoreau asked, if worldly possessions didn't occupy our thoughts? What and whom could we attend to if we stopped attending only to ourselves?

Humble solitude has its virtues, or, for Thoreau, *is* a virtue: it allows a person to see things and people more clearly. As Robert Richardson noted in his biography of Thoreau, his "venture [at Walden and the Estabrook] was in no sense a retreat or withdrawal. He himself thought of it as a step forward, a liberation, a new beginning."[33] Thoreau and Blood maintained their distance from society in order to gain a critical vantage point on it, but also to reevaluate what is, at once, most personally significant and universally true about life. This philosophical move traces its origins back to the ancients: to Diogenes the Cynic, who chose to spend his life in a barrel on the margins of society. Society was not an enlightening force but rather a deeply corrupting one—it limited what an individual could understand. When Diogenes was asked about his country of origin, he famously claimed not to have one. Existentially speaking, he's right. Where one lives, what patriotic commitments one has, what social networks bind and gird the life of an individual—all of these are largely arbitrary. Of course, when one is living in the midst of society, it is difficult to recognize the constraints. But in a barrel, in a woodshed, people are not bound to any discrete political role. The "home" of Diogenes or Perez Blood can be quite isolating, but also liberating, and ultimately—ironically—humanizing.

Thoreau and Blood believed they were citizens of the cosmos at large—"cosmopolitan" in the most literal sense of the word. This is the other, largely forgotten side of ancient cynicism: the suspicion of all things organized gives way to the belief that human beings are, in fact, deeply and universally related—tied together not by convention but by nature. Institutions may be corrupt and corrupting, but the true danger of societal constraints is that they place false boundaries between groups. On one side of cynicism, then, is the critical, or negative. On the other is hope—hope for a community that transcends any particular provincial loyalty. Cynicism downplays our traditional attachments to religion, economics, and politics. In so doing, it frees us to realize the bonds that exist beyond those self-imposed borders. The cynic looks like the outcast and the lawbreaker, but appearances are often deceiving. As Thoreau writes, "He who lives according to the highest law is [in] one sense lawless."

At the time that Thoreau communed with the "inner form" of Perez, he delivered, for the first time, his lecture "Walking," inspired by his perambulations across Blood Farm. It became his favorite essay, one that he would revise a dozen times before his death in 1862. Wildness and wolves are focal points of "Walking." Civilized society should never forget its rugged origins in the hidden woods surrounding Wolf Rock. "The story of Romulus and Remus being suckled by a wolf is not a meaningless fable," Thoreau wrote. "The founders of every state which has risen to eminence have drawn their nourishment and vigor from a similar wild source. It was because the children of the Empire were not suckled by the wolf that they were conquered and displaced by the children of the northern forests who were."[34] Such passages give rise to the standard interpretation of Thoreauvian individualism: Thoreau is advocating a form of liberty, but not the sort embodied in the military ethos of the Revolution or the civilizing tendency of the Founding Fathers. In "Walking," Thoreau aims "to speak a word for Nature, for absolute freedom and wildness, as contrasted with a freedom and culture merely civil—to regard man as an inhabitant, or a part and parcel of Nature, rather than a member of society."[35] This was the absolute freedom that both Thoreau and Perez, following in the footsteps of the earliest American Bloods, found in the Estabrook or walking on Carlisle Road. This longing for wildness stood against the business of partitioning and exploiting the land that had taken hold of New England society in the 1850s. Thoreau writes in "Walking":

> Nowadays almost all man's improvements, so called, as the building of houses and the cutting down of the forest and of all large trees, simply deform the landscape, and make it more and more tame and cheap. A people who would begin by burning the fences and let the forest stand! I saw

the fences half consumed, their ends lost in the middle of
the prairie, and some worldly miser with a surveyor looking after his bounds, while heaven had taken place around
him, and he did not see the angels going to and fro, but
was looking for an old post-hole in the midst of paradise.
I looked again, and saw him standing in the middle of a
boggy Stygian fen, surrounded by devils, and he had found
his bounds without a doubt, three little stones, where a
stake had been driven, and looking nearer, I saw that the
Prince of Darkness was his surveyor.[36]

Surveying devils and profiteers had taken over the woods
surrounding Concord, and Sumner Blood, Perez's cousin, was
one of them. Sumner was not one for walking, in the Thoreauvian sense of the word. The man had a large family and an
even larger estate that stretched toward Sudbury, to the south
of Perez's house. In 1852, Thoreau reports, "Mr. Blood cut off
his woodlot on Pomciticut Hill winter before last," and he lamented that "this act has more results than he wots of. It is an
ill wind that blows nobody any good";[37] there was some small
recompense in the fact that these denuded hillsides would bear
new blueberries and hackberries, but a distinct loss of wildness
pervaded Thoreau's reflection. Four miles to the north, however, Sumner's secluded cousin held a stand of primitive oaks
that remained intact.

THE LAST YEARS of Perez Blood's life disappeared, like so
many trees of the Estabrook, in silence. As his health declined,
his unmarried sisters assumed his care, and the three of them
lived out their remaining time together. Roads are meant to

connect two or more towns, but in the 1850s, Carlisle Road became the road to nowhere. In Thoreau's words, "Road—that old Carlisle one—that leaves towns behind; where you put off worldly thoughts; where you do not carry a watch, nor remember the proprietor; where the proprietor is the only trespasser,—looking after his apples!—the only one who mistakes his calling there, whose title is not good; where fifty may be a-barberrying and you do not see one. It is an endless succession of glades where the barberries grow thickest, successive yards amid the barberry bushes where you do not see out."[38]

Perez Blood died in 1855, at the age of seventy, bringing a life of solitude that verged on loneliness to an end. This was the self-imposed sequestration of a man whose expansive family toggled between engagement and separatism. His father, Thaddeus, had been a mainstay of the Concord community, had documented the most pivotal moment of colonial life, and was memorialized at the founding of a new nation. Perhaps Perez lacked his father's ambition, or perhaps he realized that conventional forms of ambition might preclude the simple freedoms of walking in the woods or peering into the night sky. Perez was—willingly—an outlier. "If you are ready," Thoreau wrote, "to leave father and mother, and brother and sister, and wife and child and friends, and never see them again—if you have paid your debts, and made your will, and settled all your affairs, and are a free man—then you are ready for a walk." Just go. Don't look back. Perhaps only then will you see something that you've been searching for or, more likely, simply overlooked.

American transcendentalists were obsessed with sight, with seeing things in multitude and at magnitude, as clearly as possible. Emerson directs our attention to the workings of nature but also the inner realities of our mind and heart. Look harder.

Catch sight of more. Thoreau trained his vision on his walks through the Estabrook, and in the remote woodshed of Perez Blood. A telescope is an invitation to see the natural world anew, to see exactly the same reality from a wholly different vantage point. Thoreau's interaction with Perez Blood offered a similar existential invitation: for him to see the inner, noble form of a seemingly common man. To understand that there are many equally honest ways to see the world, to see multiple aspects of the universe at once, to consider the possibility that one's current point of view is not exclusive or exhaustive—this is the transcendentalist's guiding impulse. After his interaction with Blood, Thoreau wrote of this double vision that "we noticed that it required a separate intention of the eye, a more free and abstracted vision . . . there are manifold visions in the directions of every object."[39] This was the lesson of Perez Blood. The most important part of a telescope is the aperture—the opening—which collects light from the night sky. The light is there—everywhere. One just needs a lens of the proper size.

On June 2, 1856, Thoreau took Emerson to attend the estate auction of his old friend Perez Blood. According to Thoreau, there was only one object of note: a refracting telescope, which "sold for fifty-five dollars."[40] At some point, the original price of the looking glass had been revealed or, just as likely, fabricated. The auctioneer announced it was originally priced at "ninety-five plus ten."[41] Clearly, the value of stargazing had depreciated in the course of forty years. The money from the sale of the telescope might have been passed along to Perez's unmarried sisters, one of whom lived on into her nineties. But perhaps this money had another use.

In the town records of Concord, there remains an improbable fact regarding the will and estate of Perez Blood. In 1718, at the behest of a small landowner, Peter Wright, a fund of three hundred dollars was established for the care of the poor of Concord and the surrounding area. This was the beginning of the Silent Poor Fund, which was dedicated to "deserving persons, who from age or other cause are able to earn only a partial support and who thus are unable to come upon the town."[42] In the next two hundred years, the fund grew modestly to ten thousand dollars. In 1860, there had been eleven notable contributions and dozens of nominal donations from wealthy Concord families. And there was one lump-sum gift that dwarfed the rest—the twelve hundred dollars from the sale of a remote woodlot, once owned by Perez Blood. Blood, the astronomer and recluse, would remain the principal benefactor of Concord's silent poor.[43] Though he was himself childless, he found a way to nurture the most vulnerable, who often are forced to the very outskirts of town.

PART III

PURSUIT

THE MACHINIST ≣

Hunger drives even the wolf from the forest.

—RUSSIAN PROVERB[1]

WHEN ONE CONSIDERS "LIFE, LIBERTY, AND THE pursuit of happiness," it is easy to think that the phrase consists of three, rather than four, interlocking parts. The "pursuit" usually falls out of the discussion, but it didn't for the Blood family as it expanded throughout the nineteenth century. In the 1840s, as Perez spent his final days considering the cosmos through a telescope, a younger Blood was setting off to traverse an unexplored continent.

Aretas Blood was born into poverty in Windsor, Vermont. He was a year older than Thoreau. Some of the hereditary lines of the Blood family are circuitous, but this one is not: Aretas was a direct descendant of Thomas Blood, the British ruffian turned courtier, so it's probably no surprise that he wasn't going to let the accident of a lowly birth determine his future. His is a classic American rags-to-riches story, the tale of how a common blacksmith and "job hand" came to own one of the largest locomotive companies in America and electrify a nation. Yet the life story of this machinist, like those of many other American Bloods, is two-sided. It is obviously a tale of triumph in the face of adversity, but Aretas's manic pursuit of success left untold casualties in its wake.

IT WAS 1816, and those who survived remembered it as "the poverty year" or "the year without a summer"[2] in New England.

On June 8, it began to flurry in Boston. When the last flakes settled, the town of Cabot in central Vermont recorded eighteen inches of snow. Local farmers in nearby Weathersfield, who had shorn their sheep earlier in the spring, tried in vain to reattach the fleeces with twine, but most of the naked animals died. Birds froze to death in the barren fields. Crops grew at a glacial pace, making them prone to frost. At the end of June there was a spike in temperatures—through the nineties in most New England towns—and hopes rose. Perhaps the harvest would not be wholly ruined after all. But then a wind from the Great Lakes blew in: the corn in much of New Hampshire and the beans and squash in Maine were destroyed in July. The grasses failed to grow, so hay was never threshed, and animals went hungry.[3]

It snowed again in late August, but it scarcely rained a drop. Parched woodlands in Vermont and New Hampshire burned with abandon and smoke obscured the sun. Even when the smoke cleared, a dim haze, or "dry fog," coated the atmosphere, turning all things a dusky crimson. The editor of the *Vermont Journal* wrote: "Never before in this vicinity (had the weather) appeared more gloomy and cheerless than at present. It is extremely cold for the time of year, and the drought was never before so severe."[4]

The year 1816 was not a good one to be pregnant, but Roxellena Blood was indeed carrying a child. She began to show just as the June snow arrived, as her Weathersfield neighbors took drastic, and largely futile, measures to save their flocks. In such times, people had stark choices to make. Farmers could eat their crops now and survive, or save them to seed in the coming season if they were lucky enough to survive. They could feed their cattle the remaining oats and corn, or hoard what they could for themselves. They could move west to Ohio or south to Virginia, or they could remain in New England. Roxellena and her husband, Nathaniel Blood, decided to stay. Nathaniel was a direct descendant of the Puritan James Blood, the original owner of the manse in Emerson's Concord. Roxellena was the daughter of Isaac Procter, a soldier in the Revolution. Both of them were tried-and-true New Englanders and they weren't about to be scared off by ominous snowfall or even drought. Roxellena would just have to give birth in the growing wasteland of "the poverty year."

By September, however, as she entered her final month of pregnancy, the temptation to take flight was great. The Boston author Samuel Goodrich visited the northern counties of New Hampshire and remarked, "At last a kind of despair seized upon the people. In the pressure of adversity, many persons lost their judgment, and thousands feared or felt that New England was destined, henceforth, to become part of the frigid zone."[5] At this moment of desperation, more than fifteen thousand Vermonters journeyed westward in search of milder climes; those who held out in this frigid zone were reduced to gathering wild turnips, nettles, and hedgehogs to sustain themselves through the winter. On September 28, a "black frost" darkened the last of Nathaniel Blood's remaining crops. Ten days later, in

Aretas Blood

the midst of this disaster, Roxellena gave birth to their only son—Aretas.[6]

Aretas Blood spent his life girding himself against the vagaries of fortune. The summer of 1816 had, in the words of Washington Irving, "filled the imagination [of New Englanders] with dreams and horror and apprehension of sinister and dreadful events."[7] For Aretas, the entire point of life was to hold these events at bay as long as possible. There remained, however, a question regarding the best method of resistance. His neighbors in rural Vermont had ideas: the dramatic shift in weather and the misery that it wrought was a reflection of divine will, a punishment for a culture that had lost its way. Aretas grew up at a time when farmers still earnestly prayed for good weather. If the rain didn't come or the sun didn't shine, it was because they weren't praying hard enough. Preachers in New England often climbed their steeples to ring the bells in a thunderstorm, believing the sound might ward off evil spirits. An Enlightenment commitment to science and reason might have given average Americans better comfort in the face of environmental crisis, but meteorological events were still regarded as only proximate causes of human suffering. Many people held that sunspots—detected in 1816—were responsible for the cooling of the earth; others believed that the great solar eclipse of 1806 had permanently dampened the warmth of the sun; but nearly every American at the time believed these natural events were ultimately signs from God.

Aretas Blood was raised to believe that in order to live, one must be good. Survival was also keyed to the happy coincidence that "being good" in Puritan New England was inextricably plaited to working hard. Aretas spent his youth on Nathaniel's family farm doing just that. This was not the expansive Blood Farm of Massachusetts but a modest subsistence lot that provided for his immediate family and a few of his neighbors. By one account, "[Aretas's] home life was simple, frugal, and their [sic] was a goodly portion of work to be performed by all members of the family."[8] Unlike that of Thaddeus and Perez Blood, Aretas's formal education was meager: boys reared in the northern countryside would work whenever farming was possible and study only when it was not. In the winter months, when his father's fields lay fallow, he "obtained his early literary education in the common schools of the time, which were of brief terms and generally taught by indifferently educated teachers."[9] There would be no "later" literary education for Aretas, yet he managed to acquire a degree of common sense that eluded many of his neighbors in Windsor—it was not sufficient, he learned, to simply work hard. It was necessary to work intelligently. Climbing a steeple in a lightning storm to guard against deadly forces was foolhardy. So too, it turned out, was toiling on his father's farm. "It is not enough to be industrious; so are the ants," wrote Thoreau to a friend. "What are you industrious about?"[10] For Aretas, that was precisely the question.

The year without a summer exposed the inherent instability of fending for oneself in New England. Subsistence living was always exactly one bad season away from death, and this was the realization that underwrote the Industrial Revolution of the 1820s. It wasn't merely that individuals garnered higher wages in the factories and textile mills of Lowell and Manchester, but these institutions, coupled with the modern banking system, reflected an efficiency and robustness that subsistence farming sorely lacked. They, quite literally, were able to weather great storms.

There were, and remain, three effective ways to face a natural disaster. Individuals can make a stand but adjust the way they interact and cooperate. They can develop new technologies that address danger and scarcity. Or they can take flight. Incorporate, invent, or flee—these are the options. Aretas proved that one did not have to go to college to grasp this point. He became transfixed by the single invention that more than any other embodied the survival and progress of the nineteenth century: the legendary "iron horse."

The term "iron horse" was popularized after the Rainhill Trials, held on one mile of level track outside Merseyside, England, in October 1829. The trials were meant to settle a rather nasty argument over what sort of machine should haul cargo and passengers on the nearly completed Liverpool and

Manchester Railway. More specifically, the mechanical and civil engineer George Stephenson had a hypothesis that the trials were meant to test: he claimed that his locomotive, driven solely by steam, could outpace a horse-driven engine, known as the Cycloped, a sadistic-looking device in which the animal was driven to death on a treadmill that powered two axles. In the days before the trial, Stephenson wrote: "Locomotives shall not be cowardly given up. I shall fight for them until the last. They are worth the conflict!"[11] The outcome of the immediate battle was decisive: Stephenson's Rocket triumphed, maintaining the breakneck speed of nearly fourteen miles an hour. He did not invent the modern steam locomotive, but by many accounts, Stephenson "perfected" it. In the months that followed, Stephenson invited the writer and actress Fanny Kemble to join him on a train ride outside Liverpool, hoping, no doubt, that she would popularize what still struck many as an alien mode of transportation. Kemble obliged, writing an account that secured the machine's iconic status as an indefatigable "mare . . . that [she] was rather inclined to pat."[12] The mechanical beast "goes upon two wheels," Kemble explained, "which are its feet, and are moved by bright steel legs called pistons, these are propelled by steam, and in proportion as more steam is applied to the upper extremities (the hip points I suppose) . . . the faster they move the wheels. The reins, bit and bridle of this wonderful beast is a small steel handle . . . The coals, which are its oats, were under the bench, and there was a small glass tube . . . which indicates when the creature needs water."[13] This was the publicity of Stephenson's dreams, and railways, both freight and passenger, sprang up across the United Kingdom.

In the year of the Rainhill Trials, the first English steam locomotive, the Stourbridge Lion, arrived in America, unloaded at the foundry at Cold Spring, New York. In what is considered the first poem in America on steam locomotion, written in 1836, Samuel Smith put his finger on the indomitable nature of such a machine: "Your noblest steeds of flesh and blood / Are soon with toil o'erdone / But wheels impelled by fire and flood / For ever may roll on."[14] Living things subsist but temporarily on food, but trains run perpetually on heat and water. When the Lion arrived in New York, there wasn't space to test the machine, but thousands of people came to watch when "this critter," as some called it, was placed on blocks and its wheels taken for a spin. The Lion made its first successful run in August on the Delaware and Hudson line, but, as Mr. Stephen Torrey remarked, in the process "Alva Adams had his arm blown off while firing the [starting] canon."[15] Human suffering, however, was only a minor setback in the inevitable destiny of technological progress. The American iron horse was born.

In 1828, the Baltimore and Ohio Railroad cut a swath through the Appalachian Mountains and laid the rail that initiated a journey westward at breakneck speed. By 1832, it became clear that American manufacturers would have to compete with importation of more powerful foreign locomotives, and it was in this year that the seventeen-year-old Aretas Blood set out to make his fortune. "Shun bad company; try to please your employers,"[16] Roxellena Blood instructed her son as he left his Windsor home to become an apprentice to a nearby blacksmith. He later reflected that any success he had enjoyed in life could be traced to his mother's teachings. Aretas worked in the local forge for two and a half years, just long enough to entertain higher ambitions. He did please his employers—very much, in fact. They called him indefatigable and loyal. But

Aretas, like so many other American Bloods, also harbored the not-so-secret desire to please himself.

THE BASICS OF ironworking had not changed a great deal over its six-thousand-year history. It still consisted of fire, hammer, and anvil. What changed so dramatically during Aretas's lifetime was its economy of scale. No longer were five-pound hammers wielded exclusively by the fragile arms of men. The hammers of the future were heavier—four hundred pounds heavier—and attached to shafts affixed to cranks embedded in machines. The crucibles used to refine ore became larger and hotter—blast furnaces of the 1830s were so mammoth that many of them sank into the damp Vermont soil, but those that didn't yielded a ton of iron a day. The majority of ironworkers in Blood's time were not blacksmiths, in the traditional sense of producing finished pieces that they could own and then sell. Instead they were expendable parts—like so many cogs and gears—in a vast mechanical system that converted ore to bloom to billets to bar iron.

Life in a nineteenth-century foundry was like something out of Dante's *Inferno*: being burned, crushed, or flayed wasn't an eventuality but an inevitability. At the iron pour stations, the conditions were so intense that workers regularly collapsed of heat exhaustion. Those who managed to stay hydrated might urinate in their pants to remain cool. The foundry was, however, slightly different from Dante's nightmare. The victims in the *Inferno* were largely responsible for their miseries. Generally speaking, the men and young boys—some only nine years old—working in the foundries were not. "In so far as machinery dispenses with muscular power," Karl Marx wrote, "the labor of children was . . . the first result of the capitalist application of machinery!"[17] All these ironworkers, young and old, performed simple repetitive tasks, which meant that they were largely interchangeable within the foundry, and also expendable. There was something especially tragic about the modern-day Vulcan, who for generations stood at the peak of muscular perfection. No longer, Marx explained:

> Working in moderation he is in fact in one of the best human positions, physically speaking. But we follow him to the city or town and we see the stress of the work on that strong man, and what then is his position in the death-rate of his country . . . he is made to strike so many more blows, to walk so many more steps, to breathe so many more breaths in the day . . . He meets the effort; the result is . . . he dies at 37 instead of 50.[18]

Aretas could easily have lived and died this way, but he didn't. He anticipated the expansion of his potentially deadly business, and grasped a rather sophisticated philosophical point that was made by many theorists in the 1840s, most notably by Marx in his theory of modern capitalism. Capitalism is always in search of greater efficiency, a way of producing more for less. Efficiency depends on establishing economies of scale. Modern economies of scale are maintained only through a division of labor and specialization in which each worker plays a different role in production, but no worker plays all roles at once. In a response to the English philosopher-economist John Stuart Mill, Marx argued that this division of labor radically altered the relationship between individuals and the objects they manufactured. In the eighteenth century, when the economy was still driven by the work of individual farmers and craftsmen, production was a meaningful enterprise for workers. In Marx's words, "In my production I would have objectified my individuality, its specific character, and, therefore, enjoyed not only an individual manifestation of my life during the activity, but also, when looking at the object, I would have the individual pleasure of knowing my personality to be objective, visible to the senses, and, hence, a power beyond all doubt."[19] In other words, workers could own, and identify with, the fruits of their labors. In turn, when they sold their goods, they could take satisfaction in, and payment for, something that they alone had produced. In industrialization, however, Marx argued that "agricultural folk [were] first forcibly expropriated from the soil, driven from their homes, turned into vagabonds, and then whipped, branded and tortured by grotesque terroristic laws into accepting the discipline necessary for the system of wage labour."[20] The division of labor changed the nature and meaning of work, according to Marx, and was the single root cause of modern alienation.

In *Capital*, Marx explained that "it is clear that a worker who performs the same simple operation for the whole of his life converts his body into the automatic, one-sided implement of that operation."[21] This sort of specialization leads to efficiency but also strips workers of the ability to determine their current circumstances or future prospects. In modern capitalist systems, "machine-workers," as Marx put it, are alienated both from the objects they manufacture—since they have no claim over the finished product—and from the process of production that traditionally gave them a sense of a "job well done." The wealth they create through their collective labor was never theirs to enjoy. Instead, profits flowed exclusively to the owners of the factory, who converted them into capital expenditures, further expanding manufacturing and perpetuating the exploitation of their workers.

Marx observed that the means of production in this system would necessarily have radically divergent meanings for two different classes of people in the modern world: "On the one hand, the production process incessantly converts material wealth into capital, into the capitalist's means of enjoyment and his means of valorization. On the other hand, the worker always leaves the process in the state that he entered it—a personal source of wealth, but deprived of any means of making that wealth a reality for him."[22] The young Aretas made a conscious decision regarding his place in this production cycle.

By one early twentieth-century account, Aretas mastered the "sturdy calling" at the forge by the age of twenty, and then "turned to something a little broader, which gave him more opportunity for the use of his mechanical and inventive mind, and became a machinist."[23] A machinist was substantially different from an average "machine worker." A machinist, among other things, designed and fabricated the machines that common workers used. More generally, a machinist was the artist-scientist of the ironworking world. He (machinists were almost always men) possessed varying degrees of skill in planning, boring, shaping, slotting, but especially lathing and measuring finished pieces of metallurgy. Such an artisan was unique or at least not entirely fungible. Simon Winchester observed that the Industrial Revolution—and steam locomotion specifically—would have been substantially delayed were it not for the obsessive precision of a machinist, John "Iron Mad" Wilkinson, who finally sized and fitted the leaky pistons on James Watt's steam engine. Efficiency was a function of the division of labor,

but in some cases, it was simply a matter of greater technical precision. Aretas had something of Wilkinson's obsession.
Blood's hometown of Windsor would become the birthplace
of modern precision manufacturing in the United States and
the home of the Robbins and Lawrence Armory and Machine
Shop, erected in 1846, which is today the American Precision
Museum. Blood's life as a machinist, however, predated Robbins and Lawrence. In 1840, at the age of twenty-four, he set
off for the West in hopes of finding opportunities that the satu-
rated manufacturing markets of New England could no longer
afford.[24]

EVANSVILLE, INDIANA, like Aretas, had great expectations, so he traveled there. In the decade following the disas-
trous year of 1816, Indiana's population had quadrupled and
it remained a promised land for many New Englanders in the
first half of the century. In the 1830s, Evansville had initiated
the construction of the world's longest ditch—a four-hundred-
mile canal that ran from the Great Lakes to Toledo, and into
the rivers that ran down to Evansville, just outside Louisville,
Kentucky.[25] Aretas, unlike some of his Blood brethren, was not
a ditchdigger, and he expected—quite rightly—that steam locomotives would sooner or later make the canal network cover-
ing big parts of the United States obsolete. In fact, the canal
bankrupted the state of Indiana and for many years failed to
accomplish its most basic function of holding water. Had Aretas
remained in Indiana, he'd have been involved in the successful completion of the Wabash and Erie Canal in 1853, but he
might have also noted that the Evansville and Crawfordsville
Railroad rendered it basically useless.[26]

In the summer of 1841, after just a year in Evansville, Aretas returned to New England, settling in the village of North Chelmsford, Massachusetts, on the edge of the original Blood Farm. The American Bloods spread thick through the Merrimack Valley and Aretas felt at home, at least for a time. After the banking collapse of 1837, even the most frugal or modest citizens worried about making money. In the month of Blood's return, a young Henry Thoreau, living six miles to the south, spent his time shoveling manure for seventy-five cents a day, and took up residence at the Emerson household, earning his board by gardening and teaching his mentor how to tend an orchard. This was an economic necessity rather than a high-minded choice. Life was slightly easier for Blood, who found work at the small foundry in Chelmsford, but this was not the sort of vocation that Aretas envisioned: he was, as a common machine worker, once again on the wrong side of Marx's economic analysis, on the edge of exploitation. Soon he moved north, to the Locks and Canals Company at Lowell, where he began to find a more central place in America's Industrial Revolution.[27]

TODAY THE CITY of Lowell in northern Massachusetts is a wistful, semi-dilapidated town, a shell of its former self. But when Aretas arrived in 1842, it was in its heyday, the largest manufacturing center in the country and, not long after, the world. Its streets, lined with trees and flowers, radiated from St. Anne's, the Gothic stone church at the center of town, leading to mills and shops, boardinghouses and public gardens. At the time, Lowell housed eight thousand textile workers and was the eighteenth-largest city in the United States.[28] Thoreau, who watched Lowell bloom, noted how quickly the transformation occurred: "[The rivers of] Pawtucket and Wamesit, where the Indians resorted in the fishing season, are now Lowell, the city of spindles and Manchester of America, which sends its cotton cloth round the globe. Even we youthful voyagers had spent a part of our lives in the village of Chelmsford, when the present city, whose bells we heard, was its obscure north district only, and the giant weaver was not yet fairly born. So old are we; so young is it."[29]

When the textile industry at Lowell was born in the late 1830s, so too was the hope that modern manufacturing would not be wholly antithetical to human flourishing. Charles Dickens, who visited Lowell in the year of Blood's arrival, made a comparison between Lowell and the manufacturing centers of England. There was no contest: "The contrast would be a strong one, for it would be the difference between Good and Evil, the living light and the deepest shadow."[30] Most of the women who worked in the textile mills—"mill girls," as they were termed, from the ages of fifteen to thirty-five—were genuinely happy to be part of what became known as the Lowell System of industrial labor. There was much to love about their condition: independence, camaraderie, housing, educational opportunities, and rare cash salaries (many machine workers were paid exclusively in store credit). The Lowell System was put in place to minimize the dehumanization and alienation that Marx had predicted, and for the most part, at least for the time being, it worked in the textile mills. Aretas Blood spent a year in Lowell before taking up permanent employment at the Essex Company Machine Shop in the nearby town of Lawrence, but he gleaned lasting lessons from the Lowell System. He was on the verge of becoming a capitalist, but Lowell, at least in theory, demonstrated that not all capitalists were created equal. In practice, the city reflected a deep tension that Aretas came to know firsthand: the profits of industry came at potentially staggering human costs. Most industrialists of the time would be driven by two competing—one might argue mutually exclusive—objectives: to maximize efficiency but also to maintain a clear moral bearing.

Hired as a job hand or foreman at the Essex shop in Lawrence, Blood became a vital force in an industrial behemoth.[31] Four hundred feet long, sixty feet wide, and four stories high, the factory dwarfed the surrounding neighborhood and stood starkly against the gently rolling hills surrounding Lawrence. Three of the floors were devoted to ironwork and the fourth to designing and patternmaking. Twenty furnaces burned, many of them around the clock.[32] In the 1830s, the Essex Company dammed the Merrimack River and constructed the canals and locks at Lawrence, but in 1843, around the time of Blood's arrival, the company began contracting work for the construction of some of New England's first locomotives. Blood was responsible for manufacturing the "light parts" of the iron horse: shafts, gears, and wheels, all of them requiring fabrication with fine-grained precision.

Foremen like Blood were hired to produce a given machine or gear set and could use the factory's various assets as they saw fit, managing as many as a dozen workers at a time. The massive stone building of Essex was heated by steam and lit by gas, conditions that allowed Blood to extend the workday of his laborers through the frigid darkness of winter. Aretas wasn't a slave driver but he was notoriously exacting, a man of "indomitable energy" who would be compared to the Union general Ulysses S. Grant.[33] Nearing thirty, Blood began to look the part of a modern Titan—attractive deeply set eyes, a square jaw covered by a closely cropped beard, thick arms and a barrel chest that were in keeping with the atmosphere of the foundry. He had a certain impatience with book learning and employed men at Essex who had apprenticed at common foundries like the one where he had cut his teeth.

At the Essex shop, Blood had his first taste of genuine profit. His workers earned a reasonable wage, and by one account his "own experience in searching for work made Mr. Blood considerate to those in similar circumstances," but he drew an income far larger than his men on the floor of the factory.[34] Exponentially larger, in fact: within five years Aretas had saved enough money to purchase a factory of his own, which is exactly what he did, teaming up with the superintendent Benjamin Bailey to form Vulcan Iron Works of Manchester, New Hampshire, in the fall of 1853.[35]

Living paycheck to paycheck is only marginally better than subsistence farming, but having disposable income brings its own challenges. While Thoreau and Perez Blood kept the necessities of life to a minimum, most men of their age did not. The simple, and largely expected, act of starting a family could raise the stakes of making money to considerable heights. This was especially the case for men of Aretas Blood's new socioeconomic bracket. By the time he founded Vulcan Iron Works, Aretas had a family but not the type in which he had been raised in rural Vermont. His wife, Lavinia, and two daughters, Nora and Emma, didn't work in the traditional sense of earning wages or tending the fields. They were on the cusp of joining the American upper class. This was a mixed blessing: it spared the Blood women the exploitation that often occurred within preindustrial families, but it placed unprecedented responsibility on men like Aretas to become breadwinners. He, like so many successful men of the time, was a victim of his own overweening ambition. At the time, an onlooker in Manchester reflected that Blood "enjoyed the pleasures of home and was very fond of his family" and would join them on Sunday mornings at the Franklin Street Congregational Church in downtown Manchester, but for the most part he worked with a zeal that must have occasionally bordered on the maniacal. In an age of early bedtimes, Blood often hunkered down in his office until midnight, designing machines, writing advertisements, and keeping pace with the interminable bookkeeping of a new enterprise. The same writer who described him as a family man remarked that "if [Blood] seemed entirely absorbed in his business it must be remembered that he carried on his shoulders a great responsibility, and had the welfare of a great many people in his charge dependent on his good judgment."[36] Blood rarely asked for help. He never employed a secretary and kept his own meticulous books.

As the superintendent of the Vulcan shop, Aretas managed more than a hundred hands on Machine Row in Manchester's booming industrial district. Unlike Essex, Vulcan was solely dedicated to the production of trains. Blood knew that this specialization constituted a high-risk strategy that could result in untold wealth or complete disaster. A year later, Blood folded his business into Manchester Locomotive Works and bought shares in the newly incorporated factory. By 1857, he owned the company and managed three hundred ironworkers. One word described Aretas's business model: bigger. Not only did the factory need to expand, but the engines it produced were pointedly oversized. First-generation locomotives were relatively diminutive machines, effective for transporting people and dry goods, but not much else. Aretas knew that engines had to become exponentially more powerful in order to conquer the nation. Aretas set up one of the largest machine shops in the world—a six-acre block of buildings along Canal Street in Manchester— which was supposed to produce pulling machines measured not in pounds but in tons. Blood's enthusiasm as an industrialist was visionary, in other words, as well-founded as it was dangerous.[37]

Though the 1840s are known as the Railway Age it wasn't until the following decade, in the years that Blood expanded his business, that imperialist policies and technological progress in the United States began to underwrite the construction of the transcontinental railroad. Northern and Midwestern states, led by New York, made the conscious decision to unify their transportation systems, and by 1860 had created a network of track that connected every major city east of the Mississippi. Farms, arranged concentrically around depots, sprang up in the Corn Belt—in Ohio, Indiana, and Iowa—and became the principal agricultural suppliers for the manufacturing centers of New England. Rumors of the Kansas-Nebraska Act to open the West began to swirl in 1854, and by then it was already clear that Northern railroads would be the principal gateway to the new territory. To the extent that industrialists in Virginia and the Carolinas were interested in locomotives, it was only to connect inland plantations to the shipping ports on the coast. These short railways may have provided immediate revenue, but they were, literally and figuratively, dead-end lines and ran against the current of American expansionism. Cornelius Vanderbilt did not make his millions investing in such pro- vincial undertakings and neither would Aretas Blood. These magnates had an insight regarding the relationship between modern economic markets and efficient transportation systems that was articulated by the founder of modern trade theory, Frank Taussig, in 1913:

> The division of labor has been pushed farther and farther with the extension of the market consequent on cheapened transportation . . . Plows are no longer made by the village blacksmith but put together in the great factory and then broadcast over the earth. Unless it were possible so to distribute them, plows could not be made in quantities at the factory, and their [*sic*] could be no elaborate division of labor in producing them.[38]

Reliable and inexpensive transportation was the precondition for the expansion of modern markets, the abiding link between supply and ever-widening demand. Discrete businesses might come and go, but transportation would be an enduring fixture of American life and commerce.

In 1872, the Brooklyn-based artist John Gast painted *American Progress*, an allegory of American modernization in the new West: a monumental woman in flowing white, something between Lady Liberty and the Venus de Milo, leads miners and settlers west against a native throng in full retreat. "Progress," as she is usually called, flies above her white followers, a schoolbook in one hand, a telegraph line in the other. The epitome of the civilizing impulse. Communication and education, however, were not the keys to Manifest Destiny. Mechanized transportation was. Pulling up the rear in Gast's procession, or invasion, were three iron horses, led by a locomotive with the massive boiler and top-heavy stack that Blood would help to invent.[39]

But this description makes American progress and Blood's

success seem more seamless and inevitable than they actually were. In 1857, in the year of Blood's acquisition of Manchester Locomotive Works, the United States faced the greatest financial panic of the century. Gold, discovered and mined by western forty-niners—a flood of immigrants who rushed to Colorado and California in 1849—caused an economic boom in the early 1850s, but speculation outpaced the Gold Rush and banks continued to loan well beyond their reserves. Western expansion depended on railroad companies backed by federal land grants but also, more tenuously, by stock purchased on Wall Street by investors. In the fall of 1857, banks tried to rebuild their gold reserves by increasing interest rates, which radically curtailed investment to heavy manufacturing in general and the nation's upstart railroads in particular. When the SS *Central America* (its hold filled with ten tons of gold bullion, worth $500 million) sank off the Carolina coast later that year, eastern banks began to deny loans to all western industries and refused to accept currency from newly established territories. Panic, and a sustained run on the banks, ensued. Everything, including Blood's ironworks, ground to a halt. Aretas was forced to close the doors of Manchester Locomotive in 1858, laying off two hundred employees.[40]

This was clearly the moment to go out of business. Or at the very least to downsize. But Blood had other ideas. He temporarily closed his shop, but only to consolidate his assets. He was about to go on a spending spree. There was only one company that competed with Manchester Locomotive: Amoskeag Manufacturing, which occupied a sprawling complex of mills in downtown Manchester. Despite the Panic of 1857, Amoskeag was on its way to become the largest cotton manufacturer in the world, and at its height operated eight thousand spindles at a time.[41] It also produced some of America's first trains. Blood couldn't compete with, and didn't want to acquire, this textile juggernaut, but in 1859 he convinced the owners of Amoskeag to sell him a manufacturing arm of the company, the arm dedicated to steam engine production. Blood was purchasing—at a deep discount—the very business that had foundered in the financial crisis. Buying distressed assets was, for Blood, contrarian investing at its foolhardy best.

Perhaps Blood's gamble was made in the hope of becoming famously rich, but there were other, far safer ways to make money. His willingness to risk his family's fledgling fortune stemmed from an idealism he shared with many other people—workers and intellectuals alike—that transcended material concerns and the realities of the present. Blood's ultimate objective was always to pursue a more perfect union: he believed that the iron horse, if built correctly, could, by virtue of its speed and scale, bring the country together, at least demographically and economically. Even thinkers and writers who resisted the alienation of industrial life appreciated the transformative effect of steam locomotion. Thoreau grew old watching Blood's trains course the rails from Boston to Fitchburg. "I am refreshed and expanded," he reflected, "when the freight train passes me."[42] Emerson, whose long life allowed him to witness the revolution in commerce and transportation, gave voice to Blood's vision, writing in his journal in 1849 that "the locomotive and the steamboat . . . seem to have fallen as a political aid. We could not else have held the vast North America together, which we now engage to do."[43] The unity of the United States no longer rested on the courage of soldiers or the persistence of politicians, but on the perfectionism of workers and businesspeople like Aretas Blood. "A locomotive engine," Emerson noted, "must be put together as carefully as a watch."[44] Probably more carefully—since watches did not have the capacity to explode like steam boilers, killing and maiming everyone in sight.

In the earliest years of Manchester Locomotive, Blood ensured technical perfection at all costs and, according to the local newspaper, the *Manchester Union*, those costs were frequently very high. One particularly telling story circulated through the second half of the century, coming to rest on the last page (regarded as the "funnies") of a 1911 issue of *Popular Mechanics Monthly*:

> The story is told of the times of Aretas Blood and the old Manchester locomotive works that a student came to Mr. Blood once and wanted to study the business of locomotive building in his vacation days. The student came well recommended and Mr. Blood, who never had much time for these "tech" people, sent him down to the boiler shop and placed him in charge of the foreman. The old man took the "tech" man around and in the course of the inspection of the shop they came across one boiler on the inside of which was a man at work.
>
> "How does that man get out?" inquired the "tech" man.
>
> "Oh," said the venerable pilot, "he doesn't get out. We always count on losing at least one man in the building of a boiler."[45]

If this is darkly funny, it is, at least in part, because it's partially true. "Capital is dead labor," Marx reminds us, "which vampire like, lives only by sucking living labor, and lives more, the more labor it sucks."[46] Aretas, consumed by his work, intent to make good on a risky business venture, often seemed accepting of the sacrifices that his ambition might entail. As the Civil War loomed, however, it appeared that no amount of resolve could save Blood's venture.

ON APRIL 12, 1861, Confederate troops fired on Fort Sumter in the harbor of Charleston, South Carolina. In two days, the Union forces surrendered—and the Civil War began, tearing the country apart. Many Northern manufacturers, including the vast majority of the Amoskeag plant, transitioned to the production of guns and ammunition with the assumption that producing the machines of war was the only way to endure it, but Blood bided his time. The war would end, expansion would continue, and the iron horse would run again. In the end, Blood didn't have to wait out the war. Production at the locomotive works began again in 1863, in the midst of the bitter conflict, and Blood's first engine came off the line and was sold the following January. Nine more would follow that year, four of which were sold to the Union Army for use by the US Military Railroad, a War Department agency that repurposed and expanded Southern lines captured in battle. In 1865, when the Civil War ended, Blood oversaw the production of seventeen locomotives, at sixty thousand pounds an engine. By the early 1870s, the foundry's two giant furnaces on Elm Street operated around the clock, consuming 4,500 tons of coal and 1,000 cords of wood per year. Blood oversaw seven hundred workers, and production at the mills would edge toward a hundred locomotives a year.[47] One of these was the Kancamagus, a vertical steam boiler that was placed on the cog rail at the base of Mount Washington and summited the 6,200-foot mountain in 1875.

It was, and remains, one of the most prominent iron horses in America.

Aretas Blood was on the verge of becoming the wealthiest and most respected man in the Granite State, and he used his wealth as any good capitalist would: to purchase more capital. But first he infiltrated the banking industry, becoming the president of Second National Bank, the director of Manchester National Bank, and the director of First National Bank.[48] He then acquired the fire-engine department at Amoskeag Mill (where he would produce America's first horseless engine), and was named director of Ames Manufacturing (which supplied cavalry swords for America's western expansion), director of the Globe Nail Company of Boston (boasting the world's best horseshoe nail), and director of the Amoskeag Paper Mill.

At this point, Aretas could have rested on his laurels and spent the rest of his life gazing at the stars like his forebear Perez. The contrast between the two men is stark. Perez willingly moved to the outskirts of town, opted out of the grand narrative of American progress, and left behind a legacy that is all but forgotten, save perhaps to the "silent poor." Aretas, born into abject poverty, would help drive the engine of American industry in the nineteenth century and, at least at first glance, appear to trammel anyone who would stand in his way. There is, however, another side to Aretas, or at least to those most closely associated with the magnate: his wife, Lavinia, and daughters, Nora and Emma.

AFTER AN ECONOMIC downturn in 1873, Lavinia founded the Women's Aid and Relief Society, which quickly went to

work raising money for the city's first hospital. Lavinia single-
handedly funded a home for the poor and sick, and would later
lead the subscription efforts, with a donation of $25,000, to buy
the house that would be the society's base. It was very rare for
a major newspaper in the first years of the twentieth century
to eulogize the good works of a woman, but Lavinia Kendall
Blood's obituary is an exception to the rule:

> Mrs. Aretas Blood went about doing good. With great
> wealth, with social position, with a wide circle of accom-
> plished friends, with a devoted family, with everything to
> tempt her to confine her cares and activities to the fields
> in which the prosperous and happy live, and to enable her
> to command for herself luxury and ease, she turned aside
> to the unfortunate, and without neglecting her duties to
> family or society made it her mission to heal the sick, com-
> fort the distressed, clothe the naked, feed the hungry, and
> provide homes for the homeless . . . she was the good angel
> of Manchester.[49]

This "good angel" raised her two daughters, who generally
followed in their philanthropic mother's footsteps. Nora Blood
put up the money for Carpenter Library, which stood next to
the Manchester Institute of the Arts and Sciences, founded
and paid for by her sister, Emma. Both of them sponsored the
construction of two separate children's and maternity wings at
the hospital that their parents had helped erect. It is certainly
true that philanthropy was one of the few socially accepted out-
lets for wealthy women to express themselves in the late nineteenth century, and it would have been easy enough for Lavinia
and her daughters to remain at arm's length from the sick or

disadvantaged. But it is equally true that there are a variety of darker perspectives on the motives of patrician charity in the late industrial era.

During the period of Lavinia Blood's good work in Manchester, many upper-class women attempted to embody the ideals of Christian piety by becoming "charitable visitors" in the homes of the destitute. In *Democracy and Social Ethics*, Jane Addams, the founder of Chicago's Hull House, writes of the disjoint between these "daintily clad visitors" and the working-class families they sought to advise. According to Addams, the advice often centered on everyday practicalities the visitors scarcely understood—cooking, cleaning, bookkeeping, parenting, living leanly—but this didn't keep many visitors from bestowing their opinions and holding court. Clearly, Lavinia Blood took a far more hands-on approach to assistance than most visitors. What is less clear is how the Bloods thought about poverty and sickness in Manchester, and their family's role in their perpetuation. The tales of the American Bloods are tricky, often two-faced stories, and that of Aretas Blood and his family is no exception.

In her treatment of the "charitable effort," Addams observes in 1902 that "the only families that apply for aid to the charitable agencies are those that have come to grief on the industrial side . . . they are industrially ailing and must be bolstered and helped into industrial health."[50] Addams's point is that families who fell on hard times were often advised to return to work, to redouble their efforts, but there is another way of reading Addams's comment, which sheds light on the charity of Aretas Blood and his wife and daughters. Blood's mills employed hundreds of laborers, overworked employees who died before their time, men who left families without a financial future. Marx's

contemporary and coauthor, Friedrich Engels, reflects on the
paradox of modern charity in *The Condition of the Working Class in
England*, first published in Germany in 1845 and translated into
English in 1885, just in time to describe the rise of philanthropy
in the United States:

> The English capitalist class is charitable out of self-interest;
> it gives nothing outright, but regards its gifts as a business
> matter, makes a bargain with the poor, saying, "If I spend
> this much upon benevolent institutions, I thereby pur-
> chase the right not to be troubled any further, and you are
> bound thereby to stay in your dusky holes and not to ir-
> ritate my tender nerves by exposing your misery. You shall
> despair as before, but you shall despair unseen . . . this I
> purchase with my subscription of twenty pounds for the
> infirmary!" . . . It is infamous, this charity of a Christian
> capitalist! As though they rendered the workers a service
> in first sucking out their very life-blood and then placing
> themselves before the world as mighty benefactors of hu-
> manity when they give back to the plundered victims the
> hundredth part of what belongs to them![51]

This is not to suggest that the Blood women of Manchester
gave alms out of devious or malicious intent. Instead, it is to
pause long enough to consider just how ambitious this family
was, led by the calm and collected Aretas Blood.

WHEN THE CIVIL WAR ended and the institution of slavery was dismantled, the states of the former Confederacy were
thrown into economic turmoil. Reconstruction is a misnomer—

the devastation and poverty that defined the South in the years after the war initiated more than a century of racial injustice and economic inequality. On the ground, white farmers, who had worked small family plots before the conflict, could no longer sustain themselves and were forced to join the ranks of King Cotton. Freed blacks demanded property and equal rights—neither of which were granted in any meaningful way. In the fields, sharecropping became the norm, and many disaffected farmers moved to urban centers to become industrial workers. Mills, once located exclusively in New England, began to pop up on the waterways of the Carolinas. The boom was so pronounced that by the 1880s South Carolina was called "the Massachusetts of the South." This boom, however, was not synonymous with prosperity for most workers. Their bare necessities were acquired increasingly through credit from local merchants that underwrote a vicious cycle of usury, debt, and exploitation.

Enter the "robber barons": wealthy Northern industrialists who saw Southern destitution as an opportunity to expand their financial reach. The term "robber baron" is sometimes used to describe an individual of unscrupulous business tactics, but it is more often a catchall description of one who makes money—lots of money—on the backs of others. In the 1880s, as it became clear that a different kind of racial injustice and economic inequality would only deepen, Aretas Blood began to purchase land around Columbia, South Carolina. By the end of the decade, he was president of the Columbia Water Power Company, a business responsible for improving the flow of the Columbia Canal. This was the first step in a daring business venture. In March 1893, Charles K. Oliver, owner of Druid Mills in Baltimore, approached Aretas with a proposition. Oliver proposed erecting a massive four-story factory on a nearby bluff overlooking the waterway. A hundred years earlier, this location would have struck any investor as insane: mills had to be directly on the water for their motive power. But times were about to change, and Oliver promised Aretas his plan would work. He just needed some money—a million dollars (in the ballpark of thirty million dollars today). Three days later, Aretas wrote to Oliver: he would lend the money, and only agreed because the large sum accurately reflected the sheer scale of the project. Columbia Mills would be the first mill in the world to be powered by electricity.[52]

Blood was, for a time, the most important customer of the recently established General Electric Company. Sidney B. Paine, a General Electric salesman, proposed using polyphase alternating current and induction motors to increase capacity and the speed of production. The standard direct-current shunt motors sparked and fouled easily, which meant that the lint-filled factory could grind to a halt or burn to the ground. Induction motors were clean and fireproof, and promised to keep the textile machinery running smoothly, day and night. General Electric produced two 1,000-horsepower turbines, its largest to date, and placed them at the end of Blood's Columbia Canal to supply power for the fourteen 65-horsepower electric motors located throughout the mill. For better and for worse, thanks to Aretas Blood, the age of electric industry had begun in the United States.[53]

ARETAS'S HEALTH, like that of many productive people, was preternaturally good, right up to the point it turned irreparably bad. Then he more or less fell apart, like a machine with a broken spring. The year was 1897. Aretas was eighty-one. When he passed away, his loving family commissioned the sculptor Alexander Doyle to fashion a massive Romanesque mausoleum for his remains in Manchester's Valley Cemetery. Doyle was in high demand, having spent the better part of the previous decade in New Orleans, creating monuments to Confederate heroes. The mausoleum remains the largest and most ornate in the Manchester burial ground and cost the family forty thousand dollars to erect.[54] Blood's is the story of American economic mobility, an account of a man's largely self-determined journey from poverty to wealth. What sort of epilogue is appropriate for such a story?

Travel a thousand miles south from Manchester, and on the west bank of the Congaree River, in the shadow of the Columbia Mills, you will find a commemorative plaque designating the site of a former mill village of three hundred families. Rent was free, provided that a majority of the family members worked at the mills. The workday began at six a.m. and ended twelve hours later. The pay was eighty cents—a day. And you worked six and even seven days a week. The vast majority of its inhabitants lived, worked, and died in what was known as "Aretas-ville."[55]

THE SURVIVOR ≡≡≡

If ever there was a country where wolves are surpassingly abundant, it is the one we now are in.

—JOHN JAMES AUDUBON, 1850S,
WRITING FROM EASTERN MONTANA[1]

ARETAS BLOOD CONSOLIDATED HIS FORTUNE IN New England by hiring workers in the South, but his wealth was largely a function of the expansion and settlement of the American West. In the 1850s, many of his Blood relatives became the ranchers, miners, and soldiers who would attempt to tame the frontier. Others became the tavern owners, gamblers, and robbers who made the Wild West. Sometimes, the tension between civilization and wilderness emerged in a single American Blood. As they moved west, many Bloods came to understand the border as a paradoxical space, where the most vicious of beings could also be the most vulnerable. This was a lesson that Col. James Clinton Blood, cofounder of the town of Lawrence, Kansas, learned by heart. Like Aretas, James was a Vermonter, born on the outskirts of Burlington in 1819, at a time when wolves still roamed his family's backyard.[2] But through the 1840s these large predators were eradicated in Massachusetts and Vermont and the beasts moved west—like so many New Englanders—where one could make a living if they were willing to face the danger.

In 1825, the US government seized the land from thirty Native American tribes in the East and gave them a tract of what would become Kansas in return; land north of the Kansas River was given to the Delaware, land south to the Shawnee.[3] This land grant, like all Native land grants west of the Mississippi River, was temporary and contingent: when thirty million white settlers began to flood into the territory, the Native tribes were unceremoniously removed, convinced to sell their land at bargain prices. In the years that followed, settlers dispensed with the pleasantries of making a deal and simply transplanted or exterminated the Native inhabitants.

Arriving in August 1854 as part of what Blood called the "first party of Eastern immigrants to arrive in Kansas," he was among the pioneering homesteaders to settle the borderlands of the United States.[4] Blood's claim about being among the first emigrants to settle Kansas isn't exactly true, but he was among the first to settle the land for a particular reason. The New England Emigrant Aid Company was established in Boston in 1854 by Eli Thayer; it was essentially a moving company for emigrants, one with a moral and political agenda. When Congress passed the Kansas-Nebraska Act earlier in the year, the US government made it clear that the question of slavery would be settled more or less by head count: those territories with more opponents to slavery than proponents would be free states when they joined the Union. The abolitionist Thayer's dream was to send twenty thousand fellow abolitionists a year into the

James Blood of
Lawrence, Kansas

western territory, securing freedom for "all."[5] That this meant
displacing some of the three hundred thousand Native people
in the region was largely an afterthought to men like Thayer
and Blood. Blood served as an agent and scout for the company,
helping to select and purchase the lands that would become
Lawrence and Manhattan, Kansas.

Thayer's dream of a sweeping throng of abolitionists
never came to fruition—only two thousand (not twenty thousand) emigrants were "aided" in Kansas—but his rhetoric and
intent was not lost on proslavery factions in bordering states.[6]
The Civil War is typically framed as a confrontation between
the North and the South, as an ideological struggle between the
free states of the Union and the slave states of the Confederacy.
But the war, in fact, began in the West—in the violence of what

came to be called "Bloody Kansas." Lawrence, Kansas, and the town's leader, James Blood, were at the very center of it. Kansas finally became a state in 1861, but not until a vicious war had been waged—sometimes called the "Kansas civil war"—to determine exactly what sort of state it would become. It was divided between James's abolitionist party from New England and proslavery bands inspired by neighboring Missouri. The abolitionist cause headquartered at Lawrence. Both sides were armed and violent.

LIKE SO MANY major conflicts, "the bleeding of Kansas" from 1855 to 1860 began as a largely avoidable altercation. In 1855, a Free Stater, Charles Dow, was killed in a property dispute. One of his friends began to make accusations and was thrown in jail for something between slander and disturbing the peace. Of course, his Free State friends liberated him from the proslavery Sheriff Jones, and the band retreated to Lawrence. Sheriff Jones helped assemble a proslavery militia composed of a thousand Missourians who encircled the town, armed with stolen guns and a cannon.[7] That evening, a raid on Lawrence was averted (the townspeople convinced Jones they weren't harboring fugitives), but Jones was only temporarily appeased. He bided his time, identified the suspects, and hoped to find them all in Lawrence on an appointed day. In the spring of 1856, James Blood traveled to New England on business, leaving his daughter and wife behind in Kansas. Blood was in New Hampshire when he received word that a group of proslavery "rough-riders" were gathering again to raid the town.[8] Returning immediately, Blood arrived in Kansas City and hired a covered hack to take him the rest of the way.

On the way home, Blood met John Brown, the man who would become an abolitionist legend, and his sons outside their hometown of Osawatomie. The best-known portrait of Brown, held today at the Boston Athenaeum, was taken in 1856, in the year of his encounter with Blood. He is pictured, arms folded across his chest, dressed in a jet-black coat with a high, almost preacher-like collar. His lips curl down disapprovingly, and deep-set wrinkles line his mouth and weathered cheeks. Jutting black brows threaten to swallow two small but inescapable eyes. On the night outside Osawatomie, John Brown informed James Blood that his town of Lawrence had been destroyed. This turned out to be a gross exaggeration. The sack of Lawrence amounted to Sheriff Jones attempting to bombard the Free State Hotel, a symbol of the town's political leanings. The hotel resisted Jones's cannon assault, and his forces resorted to tearing it down by hand, at which point the building fell—on one of Jones's men—resulting in the only fatality of the raid.[9]

John Brown exaggerated the destruction of Lawrence to justify his own murderous intentions. When they crossed paths with the future mayor of Lawrence, James Blood, the Browns assured him that the town would be avenged in what they called a "secret mission." Blood was certainly among the first to hear of the plan; looking back, Blood recalled Brown's "wild and frenzied" insistence on secrecy. Blood was to tell no one, on any condition. Days later the secret was revealed: Brown and his men had killed five members of a proslavery faction in what was called the Pottawatomie Massacre. Led by Brown, the party of seven hacked their victims to death with broadswords, in front of their families. James Blood's Kansas was the training ground for Brown, who would garner the financial support of the backers of the Emigrant Aid Company, purchase handguns and rifles, and lead the failed raid against proslavery forces at Harpers Ferry in October 1859, an act that precipitated the Civil War.[10]

The transcendentalists who still lived near Blood Farm in Massachusetts in the 1850s supported Brown and glorified his violence. The author Franklin Sanborn was a member of the "Secret Six" committee that financed Brown's raid on Harpers Ferry, and both Emerson and Thoreau donated money to Brown when he visited Concord in 1857. In light of the attack on Harpers Ferry, Emerson attested that Brown was an "idealist." "He believed," according to Emerson, "in his ideas to that extent that he existed to put them all into action . . . We fancy, in Massachusetts, that we are free; yet it seems the government is quite unreliable. Great wealth, great population, men of talent in the executive, on the bench . . . and yet, life and freedom are not safe."[11] As the Civil War loomed, New England intellectuals began to realize that ideas had to be more closely tethered to social and political action, to the fate of individuals and their communities. Brown, in life, but especially in death, remained a touchstone for this realization. Frederick Douglass praised him, writing that "Brown loved liberty for the poor and the weak."[12] Similarly, Thoreau, in the twilight of his own short life, defended Brown to the end:

When the troubles in Kansas began, [Brown] sent several of his sons thither to strengthen the party of the Free State men, fitting them out with such weapons as he had; telling them that if the troubles should increase, and there should be need of his, he would follow, to assist them with his hand

and counsel. This, as you all know, he soon after did; and it was through his agency, far more than any other's, that Kansas was made free.[13]

James Blood, however, knew something that the intellectuals of the East did not, that Brown may have helped make Kansas free but also unspeakably bloody. The bleeding of Kansas has been called a "tragic prelude" to the Civil War, spring training for a war that pitted neighbor against neighbor. Prior to his attack on Harpers Ferry, Brown joined James Lane in leading the Kansas Jayhawkers, a group of free-state militias that raided proslavery farms and freed enslaved people throughout Missouri. The Kansas Jayhawkers plundered and burned deserted cities to the ground, attacks that lingered in the collective memory of proslavery communities in the border region. In the midst of the Civil War, Lawrence, a bastion of abolitionist sentiment, would become the principal site of reprisal for Jayhawker violence.

In his antebellum years in Lawrence, James Blood fashioned himself a pragmatist, but not in the strict philosophical sense: he wanted his town, first and foremost, to survive, and counseled moderation between the zealotry of Brown and Lane (he openly despised the latter) and the proslavery forces that threatened Lawrence from the east. He was respected by both sides and, unlike so many of his Blood relatives, had a healthy respect for the rule of law. Nearing forty, the man

John Brown

cut a solid figure: tall, athletic, respectably dressed, with deep-set eyes and a dark bushy beard that enveloped his mouth and faded into white at its edges. He was known as "the Colonel" to the early settlers of Lawrence and he did his part to keep up a martial appearance. By the end of the 1850s, many Blood relatives had followed James into the Kansas territory, which served as the entrance to the Oregon and California Trails. Many of the Kansas Bloods occupied the borderland between civilization and wilderness. Today, Kansas is not a particularly wild place, but in the time of the Bloods, it stood on the brink. The hamlet of Blood Creek—named for the family, not for the vital substance—located thirty miles west of Lawrence, boasted as many as thirty saloons in just a two-mile radius. James Blood largely avoided Blood Creek. The task of maintaining some sense of order in his town was going to be hard enough.[14]

In September 1856, a committee of Lawrence citizens wrote to Blood and his ally, Governor Stearns, regarding the impending conflict with the border ruffians from Missouri:

As an approaching storm of the elements, sends forth its premonitions in the low rumbling thunder, so does the coming Missouri storm, which is perhaps to deluge Kansas with rivers of blood, even now utter its prognosticating symptoms. We hear from every quarter, that the Missouri lion "is not dead, but only sleepeth"; & that it only awaits a favorable moment to make one more spring upon its intended victim. After the Presidential election, it seems almost certain that our valor will again be tested, unless vigorous preparations on our part, shall frighten the crouching tiger from his lair.[15]

The committee was right. The election of the Democratic presidential candidate James Buchanan brought about a policy of "popular sovereignty," which, at least in theory, was to allow occupants of the Kansas territory to vote on the question of slavery for the region. In practice, it led to a territorial civil war. In light of the election, citizens entreated Blood: "At least 1000 [bushels], or 2000 Sacks of Flour should be immediately transported to Lawrence: either through Missouri, or over the overland route. This amount will be absolutely necessary to sustain a long continued siege; such as we shall probably be subjected to, if invaded."[16] Additionally, five stone houses were erected at the edge of town to serve as forts in case of invasion. To be clear: war had yet to be declared. The conflict between Kansas and Missouri was more of a Hobbesian war "of all against all" that could break out at any time. On October 19, Blood was allotted three thousand dollars to secure his community, and rations and fortifications were readied.[17] It wasn't enough.

In 1859, Blood was made county treasurer, a prosaic-sounding title but one with a life-and-death significance. He was now in charge of trade between his beleaguered people and the more prosperous neighboring territories. Blood was in steady correspondence with federal authorities and officials from bordering free states, and he was not above begging. On October 10, 1860, C. W. Holder, a community leader from Bloomington, Illinois, wrote to Blood:

> In reference to the loan you speak of, I do not think it could
> be effected here, our people as you are probably aware are
> just recovering from the financial pressure of the past 3
> years, and though we have but little money, Providence

has blessed us with a bountiful crop which, (from the feeling already manifested) I doubt not our people will gladly share with their suffering brethren in Kansas . . . I hope the people of Kansas will not regard this assistance as a charity but merely as a loan from their more fortunate neighbors which I am sure will be cheerfully repaid should we ever be in a like situation. The people of Illinois will not allow their brethren in Kansas to lack for Bread or seed, but we will send you of our abundance, which we can do without injury to ourselves.[18]

Blood's Free State townspeople, while experiencing widespread economic failure, achieved highly visible political success on the question of slavery. Many politicians of the time, most notably Abraham Lincoln, understood the conflict in Kansas—culminating in a hard-won free-state constitution of 1859—as proof positive for Republican abolitionism applied to the nation as a whole. Blood was central to the passing of this constitution, which explicitly forbade slavery in the territory, and took great pride in establishing a formal state founded upon ideals. Campaigning in the Republican primaries in Leavenworth, Kansas, in December 1859, Lincoln addressed his audience:

You, the people of Kansas, furnish the example of the first application of this new policy. At the end of about five years, after having almost continual struggles, fire and bloodshed, over this very question, and after having framed several State Constitutions, you have, at last, secured a Free State Constitution, under which you will probably be admitted into the Union. You have, at last, at

the end of all this difficulty, attained what we, in the old
North-western Territory, attained without any difficulty
at all.[19]

According to Lincoln, the efforts of Kansas Republicans
stood in stark contrast to the Democratic idea of "popular sovereignty": the Republicans' approach was pointedly principled,
and they were willing to face secession for the sake of abolitionism; the Democrats' popular sovereignty by contrast amounted
to a hands-off policy that allowed local factions to form and
slowly kill each other off. In Lincoln's words, "If a house was on
fire there could be but two parties. One in favor of putting out
the fire. Another in favor of the house burning. But these popular sovereignty fellows would stand aloof and argue against
interfering. The house must take care of itself subject only to
the constitution and the conditions of fire and wood."[20] In the
end, these words did not earn Lincoln a nomination from the
Kansas Republican delegation, of which Blood was a member.
They selected an even more fervent antislavery nominee, but
Lincoln still won the general election, and at his victory speech
in February 1861, he raised a thirty-four-starred American flag,
celebrating Kansas's admission to the Union, only months after
the first Southern states began to secede.

IN THE FALL of 1861, Governor Charles Robinson, a former
leader of the Emigrant Aid Company, wrote to his longtime
friend James Blood announcing his intention to raise a regiment for the Union in the eastern counties of the new state,
with an eye toward entering Missouri, which was painfully
divided between Union and Confederate sympathizers. There

was the very real chance that if Missouri fell into Confederate hands and was allowed to secede uncontested, Lincoln might be forced to recognize the independence of the entire South. At least that was the fear shared by Blood and many others.

This possibility was averted: as James Blood assumed the position of major general for the southern militias of the state, it became clearer his opponents, centered in Missouri, remained of two minds about the political destiny of the South.[21] Missouri was a slaveholding state, but never wanted to leave the Union entirely. When Missourians called a convention to secede, they failed to garner popular support. On May 10, the secessionist governor of Missouri, Claiborne Fox Jackson, refused to muster troops against the Confederacy and was overpowered by Union forces and his own Missouri volunteers, but when the Union paraded their captives through the streets of St. Louis, proslavery mobs rioted. Twenty bystanders were killed in acts of random violence.[22]

AT FIRST GLANCE, Lawrence's prospects, and therefore Blood's, appeared almost promising. By 1862, the Union had pushed the Confederates south and west into Arkansas. At the Battle of Pea Ridge in March 1862, the Confederates made a final, unsuccessful stand to defend Missouri, but ultimately were forced to retreat.[23] The rumors, however, continued to swirl: Lawrence was going to be ransacked one way or another. The Confederates might not claim widespread victory, but their bushwhackers (partisan militia groups that ranged over Appalachia and into the Midwest) could still wreak terror on unsuspecting communities. The citizens of Lawrence had been on high alert so long for so many reasons—they knew the drill.

In the early summer months of 1863, they marshaled defenses against a threat that never materialized. At the end of July, the guards at the vulnerable edge of Lawrence were called back. This was precisely the move a Confederate bushwhacker by the name of William Quantrill had been waiting for.[24]

Compared to Blood, Quantrill was still a young man, with a boyish face and smug smile partially covered by a handlebar mustache. Born in the relative backwoods of Ohio in 1837, he survived a childhood with an abusive father, Thomas Quantrill, who mercifully died of tuberculosis when his son was seventeen. Merciful in part: Thomas left his family in crippling debt, which pushed William into hard manual work and a life of crime. He killed his first victim while working a late shift at a lumberyard in Mendota, Illinois, at the age of nineteen. Two years later, he joined a settler community to go west, but was promptly banished for stealing the goods that supported the community. When he joined the US Army as a teamster, he specialized in the game of poker—and that is all.[25] He migrated from Colorado to Blood's town of Lawrence, teaching at a school for a short time (the standards of education were somewhat different in the nineteenth century) before failing to adjust to the impecunious nature of the profession and returning to less morally uplifting work. Quantrill did not have any deep political leanings, just those that tipped toward his own self-interest. He had, at one point, opposed slavery, but by 1860 he had discovered a pointedly proslavery occupation: using Black freemen to gain the confidence of escaped slaves, recapturing them, and returning them to their owners for bounty.[26] It was a lucrative job, one that set the stage for William's life in the ranks of Confederate bushwhackers, or guerrilla shock troops.

Bushwhackers were, at the risk of euphemism, scoundrels.

Ex-convicts, aspiring convicts, and criminals who would never be apprehended—they ranged through the mid-Atlantic states to the Midwest, terrorizing and sometimes even destroying largely helpless communities. This is not to say that guerrillas sympathetic to the Union cause were any better. They weren't. But this story isn't about them. It's about James Blood's settlement and William Quantrill's intentions on the eve of August 20, 1863. By this point, Quantrill's reputation for brutality had earned his sisters a place in a Union prison; when the prison collapsed, killing them both, their brother invaded Kansas with "vengeance in [his] heart." In the third week of August, Quantrill gathered his forces and employed local farmers outside Lawrence to guide them over the confusing terrain under cover of night. He then killed the farmers when they no longer knew the way.[27]

Staggering casualties in battles of Gettysburg and Vicksburg in July 1863 put the Confederate army on the defensive, but that could not have mattered less to the men who assembled above Blood's home. Jesse James, the infamous outlaw of the West, had joined Quantrill in the previous year, along with his brother Franklin. Franklin was actually far more murderous than his younger, more renowned brother. The only man who rivaled Franklin's brutality was a long-haired killer called "Bloody Bill" Anderson. Bill has been described equally as a sadist and a sympathetic character who mirrored the violence of the American frontier. In any event, Franklin James, Bloody Bill, and William Quantrill were about to go to work on the town of Lawrence.[28]

All this could be seen as the comeuppance for the brutality exacted by generations of the American Bloods, some of whom bore comparison to Quantrill's bushwhackers. But I am inclined to think that the fate of Lawrence and this particular American Blood is more tragic than karmic. The Bloods participated in and perpetuated the violence and ambition that defined the making of America from its inception. James Blood knew exactly what sort of country he was trying to settle. The West is usually depicted as a place of bank robbery and stagecoach heist, but in James's day there weren't really banks or stagecoaches, just wolves. James's world was that of the Great Plains buffalo and timber wolf. Hundreds of packs moved in tandem with the waves of buffalo as they migrated from Michigan to New Mexico—right across Kansas. Each year, more than a third of all bison calves were singled out and ambushed by predators. The wolves hunted their prey. And humans hunted the wolves—and each other. The trick was to render one's quarry as defenseless as possible. White hunters in the 1860s usually started by killing two or three bison in an open field, partially butchering the animals, and then sprinkling strychnine over the open flesh. The next morning, they would collect the wolves—up to a hundred at a single site—that had dined on their poisoned supper.[29]

In the predawn hours of August 21, 1863, four hundred Confederate bushwhackers, led by William Quantrill, gathered on Hogback Ridge three hundred feet above Lawrence. When they descended, they immediately surrounded the Johnson House, a large stone structure kept by a Mr. Pickens on the west side of Vermont Street. Fourteen men of Lawrence were already inside. "All we want," Quantrill's raiders insisted, "is for the men to give themselves up and we will spare them and burn the house."[30] In 1856, in the first sacking of the town by Sheriff Jones, no citizen was killed, in part because they offered no resistance to the plundering and burning of the town:

a memory that led most of the men at the Johnson House to lay down their arms and line up on the street in front of Quantrill's force. They were robbed, beaten, and summarily executed. The guerrillas broke into a general store next door where two young clerks slept and forced the teenagers to outfit them handsomely. At which point, the well-dressed soldiers butchered the boys. This was how the Sack of Lawrence, known as Bloody Dawn or Black Friday, was carried out: take what could be taken, and obliterate the rest.[31]

When Quantrill's men came for James Blood, he was already gone. Blood lived at the base of Hogback Ridge and should have been the first to be killed. But instead of running through town, where he certainly would have been slaughtered, James fled his home and hid on the hill as the guerrilla line approached in the near darkness.[32] The bushwhackers passed without noticing him, set fire to his house, and continued their march through the town. The conflict at Lawrence wasn't a battle so much as a

Quantrill's raid of Lawrence

mass execution. By the end of the day, the town lay in cinders. Nearly two hundred unarmed men and boys had been killed.

Blood, like every other man who survived the Lawrence Massacre, stayed in hiding. The heroes of Lawrence were its women, who dragged their stabbed sons and half-flayed husbands to safety and fought the fires as quickly as they were set, managing to save a handful of houses, including Blood's.[33] Members of the Blood family were used to setting the terms of a fight, yet James was forced to flee, one of the few survivors of a murderous hunt. The seal of Lawrence, Kansas, still reflects the devastation of the Bloody Dawn: a phoenix rising out of the smoldering ruins of a town.

IN THE COMING decades, Colonel Blood reinvented himself first as a bricklayer, then as lawmaker, who literally and figuratively rebuilt the city. He moved to a fine Victorian house on

Massachusetts Street, Lawrence, Kansas, circa 1856

Tennessee Avenue, a street that had been gutted in the massacre. His life became one of steady industry, and Kansas began to evolve into the wholesome American state we know today. The post–Civil War historical record of James Blood of Lawrence goes gradually dry. Blood happily watched the frontier town civilize itself. One thing, however, is certain: as James grew older and more respectable, he would have witnessed one of the most gruesome eras of American history, precipitated by the nation's self-declared civilizing mission. When Blood arrived to settle Kansas in the 1850s, lands were at least nominally purchased from local Native tribes, and Blood served as a broker for these deals. But the nature of western settlements would change dramatically during Blood's lifetime.

After the Civil War, the animus of Bloody Kansas was immediately channeled into the forcible clearing of the West of its original inhabitants; Union bluecoats were recommissioned to fight in the Indian Wars that would be waged for more than three decades in Blood's backyard. Kansas sat at the intersection of the growing conflict: to the north were the Black Hills, the ancestral hunting grounds of the Sioux; to the south the desolate prairie of Oklahoma, the semipermanent reservation land proposed by white lawmakers in Washington. When the Civil War ended, a growing number of Plains tribes—the Kiowa, Cheyenne, and Comanche—followed the remaining buffalo herds into the territories between the Arkansas River in Nebraska and the Platte River bisecting Blood's Kansas.[34] General Sherman, who turned from the Civil War to lead the campaign against the Plains tribes, explained the problem and articulated the final solution: "My opinion is that if fifty Indians are allowed to remain between the Arkansas and the Platte we will have to guard every stage station, every train, and all railroad working parties. In other words, fifty hostile Natives will check mate three-thousand soldiers. Rather get them out as soon as possible, and it makes little difference whether they be coaxed out by Indian commissioners or killed."[35]

Ultimately, the tribes of Kansas were not coaxed out of the territory. In April 1867, Governor Crawford returned from a trip to Washington to find, in his words, that "General Hancock was in the field with a handful of United States troops, and the plains of Kansas were swarming with bloodthirsty Indians."[36] On April 12, Winfield Hancock, a Union hero from the Battle of Gettysburg, charged with bringing these "Indians" under control, had invited the Cheyenne to Fort Larned, southwest of Lawrence, to broker a peace deal. When negotiations failed, he resorted to threating the chiefs: "You know very well, if you go to war with the white man you will lose . . . I have a great many chiefs with me that have commanded more men than you ever saw, and they have fought more great battles than you have fought fights."[37] A week later Hancock made good on the threats, routing a camp of Cheyenne and Lakota and burning their abandoned teepees to the ground. This was the unofficial declaration of what became known as Hancock's War, a series of increasingly bloody battles fought between the invaders and the displaced, between the trespassers and a people in search of a home.

Blood's Kansas was also the site of the rise to power of George Armstrong Custer, the unsettling icon of the conquest of the American West. Having graduated at the bottom of his class at West Point and successfully survived the Civil War, Custer was made lieutenant colonel of the Seventh Cavalry Regiment at Fort Riley, overlooking Lawrence, Kansas. When Hancock's

War came to an end with the Medicine Lodge Treaties in October 1867, many tribes were forcibly ushered into the Oklahoma Indian Territory. It was Custer's job to keep them there—and destroy those who refused to stay put. Of course, there was one insurmountable problem: the original inhabitants of the American Plains lived and flourished only by moving in tandem with the buffalo herds. And buffalo have little, yet very determined, minds of their own. Satanta, the chief of the Kiowa, responded to the proposed reservations in a way that many American Bloods would have understood: "I don't want to settle. I love to roam. There I feel happy and free, but when we settle down we grow pale and die."[38] In the late 1860s, white hunters, primarily from Kansas, moving freely across the Plains, decimated the buffalo herds, skinning the beasts and leaving the carcasses to roast and rot in the sun. This was an affront of incalculable proportions to the Native people hemmed up in government-sanctioned reservations. Between 1872 and 1874, 3.7 million buffalo were slaughtered on the Plains, only 150,000 by the tribes of the land. Satanta lamented his lack of recourse: "When I go up the river I see camps of soldiers on its banks. These soldiers cut down my timber; they kill my buffalo . . . Has the white man become a child that he should so recklessly kill and not eat?"[39] All the while, General Custer became the enforcer of this ruthless regime, one that prioritized the railroad and westward expansion above all else, most especially above the life, liberty, and happiness of a people the American government failed to recognize.

Satanta's Kiowa were unwilling to accept their fate. They could retreat, hide, rebuild, and fight, which is what they did, with tragic results in the 1870s. Newspapers from Lawrence to Philadelphia told of Lone Wolf, a Kiowa leader and friend to

Satanta, who went off the reservation in Oklahoma and disappeared with a few hundred followers into the panhandle of
Texas. Lone Wolf didn't disappear, but rather went into hiding
in Palo Duro Canyon, at the epicenter of the last great buffalo
range.[40] For the Kiowa, who had long suffered on agency lands,
Palo Duro was the promised land, an oasis of water and green-
ery that attracted and sustained the only animal that could
see a tribe through the winter. In contrast to the hunting tech-
niques of white settlers, the Kiowa, along with the Comanche
and Cheyenne they joined in the canyon, killed the fewest number of buffalo required to survive, and took pains not to waste
anything. Lone Wolf's escape to safety in 1874 was considered
an insult to the nation's civilizing mission. General Sherman
ordered two thousand troops, with artillery and repeating rifles, into the canyon, where they flushed out the camps and
killed more than a thousand ponies, the lifeline of the Native
way of life in Palo Duro. Lone Wolf and his fellow warriors
were captured and held for days in an unroofed icehouse at Fort
Sill, Oklahoma, a containment cell where they were occasionally thrown scraps of raw meat by passing US soldiers. Lone
Wolf was then transferred to a permanent prison in Florida,
where he contracted a fatal bout of malaria. Many of his fellow warriors—who had been captured in the paradise of Palo
Duro—ultimately killed themselves under the watchful eye of
the federal Indian agency.[41]

IN 1884, TWENTY-TWO elementary school students entered
the inaugural class of the United States Indian Industrial Training School in Lawrence. All of them had been taken from their
families, who were living in Kiowa, Comanche, and Cheyenne

camps. By the second semester, four hundred youngsters were brought to the school, with the express purpose of ridding them of their Native ways.

The children's hair was cut and their language forbidden. They were made to march to class, to wear uniforms, to drill, to exercise vigorously, and to master certain industrial trades. Children who objected would be placed in a small dungeon in the basement of the school. In a recent exploration of the school's archive, a pair of miniature handcuffs were found, perfectly fitted to a ten-year-old's wrists.[42] One hundred and three children died in the early years of this school that would become Haskell Indian Nations University.

A five-minute ride to the north of Haskell stands a large early Victorian house with a wraparound porch and brocaded archways, one of the finest houses in town, the onetime home of the respectable Col. James Blood.

PART IV

HAPPINESS

THE LOVERS ≣

The wolf rises in the heart.

ARETAS AND JAMES BLOOD FACED THE PRACTICAL
challenges of forging a nation, succeeding and failing in all the
quintessentially American ways. Ingenious, idealistic, morally
flawed, occasionally overreaching, they were, from beginning
to grueling end, men of action. They were engaged in the "civilizing" of a country, in the task of unifying its disparate parts
into a workable whole. The task remained, and remains, woe-
fully incomplete, but the intent and attempt were all that mattered for many of the Bloods. Some say the American mindset
underwent a similar transition in the Civil War: high-minded
ideals of personal freedom were replaced by practical plans for
progress. In the aftermath of the conflict, even Emerson admitted that it was time for unfettered individuals to place themselves at the service of society and organization. Gone were
the starry observations of Thoreau and Perez Blood; gone was
the idea that life could be lived in seclusion or freely as a noble

savage; gone was the idea that speculation could be divorced from deeds.

All of this is, in some respects, true. But it would be wrong to say that American life in the late nineteenth century was guided exclusively by practical concerns. Pragmatism arose in the 1870s—a philosophy of action and results driven by C. S. Peirce, John Dewey, and William James—but a fascinating countercurrent gathered strength in that period, defying the belief that happiness could be reduced to the habits of "normal life." America was a land of action and industry, but it also continued to be defined by an idealism that often veered, wildly, into spiritualism and mysticism. This idealism was born of a fear that the affairs of this world, the world of money, power, and fame, would overtake real life. In response, men and women—including many American Bloods—became seers and seekers, exploring the transcendental and philosophical realms as a place to tap lasting meaning.

James Blood of Lawrence, Kansas, may have contented himself with reestablishing the order of striving and surviving in everyday life, but his cousin, James Harvey Blood of St. Louis, did not. Catastrophe such as total war interrupts the routine patterns of life and rends the societal ties that usually hold us together. Of course, this can be horribly disruptive, but also, it turns out, surprisingly liberating. When the worst thing in the world occurs, and you somehow live through it, very little remains to frighten you. You can respond to crisis by clinging to some semblance of stability, by becoming more conservative, or you can go with the flow and become a radical. And this is what James Harvey Blood became. This Blood lived his short life like there was no tomorrow.

Like his cousin, James Harvey fought fiercely in the Civil War, commanding the Sixth Missouri Volunteer Infantry in the Union Army, but as the war came to an end, he did not seek to reorder the frontier. For this Blood, the conflict revealed the inherent instability of the material world. Instead of forcing it to cohere, James largely abandoned it, becoming what was known in the nineteenth century as a spiritualist, a man who believed that communing with spirits was not only possible but necessary for living a well-adjusted, *free* human life. According to Blood, the "real world"—governed by hypocritical laws, stifling conventions, and corrupting politicians—wasn't real at all but masked the spiritual realm, which had the only claim on reality. Blood was wounded several times in the war, and in April 1864 sought out treatment suitable to a man of his convictions,

James Blood,
husband of Victoria
Woodhull

visiting "a spiritual physician," a woman healer who had for many months offered her services to the ailing and infirm of St. Louis. The woman was twenty-six years old, married to a drunkard, daughter to ruthless and eccentric parents, mother to a child she described as a "half-idiot." She was also strikingly beautiful. In the middle of the appointment with Blood, she fell into a trance and, in this state, revealed that they would be married. Never mind that Blood was already married; that was beside the point. As she would later explain: "I am a free lover. I have an inalienable, constitutional and natural right to love whom I may, to love as long or short a period as I can; to change that love every day if I please."[2] James proposed on the spot. The two filed for their respective divorces, were married in the coming year, left St. Louis, and reached New York in 1867. This "spiritual physician" was none other than Victoria Woodhull, arguably the most famous and scandalous of the American Bloods.

THE STORY OF THE BLOODS can be read as a protracted, tragic history of American manhood, yet it hides a largely forgotten counternarrative: the Blood women were always very present, putting out fires, holding down the fort, quietly managing the crises that usually befell, or were instigated by, their husbands, fathers, and brothers. Blood Farm on the outskirts of Concord, with its thousands of acres, would never have been owned by Robert were it not for the dowry of Elizabeth Willard (Blood). Perez Blood would have surely died were it not for the care of his unmarried sisters. And James Harvey Blood would have been justly forgotten by history were it not for Victoria, a woman who was no mere spiritual physician but, for a time, the most notable freedom fighter in America.

Victoria was born the seventh child of Buck and Roxy Claflin, in Homer, Ohio, in 1838. Buck Claflin was, by every measure, a disappointing example of humanity: a horse-trading, swindling card shark. The closest he came to making an honest living was selling an opium-laced alcohol concoction called "Miss Tennessee's Magnetic Life Elixir."[3] "He looked like a sneak," said the anarchist Benjamin Tucker after meeting Buck many years later. In fact, he was a violent "sneak."[4] A confidant of Victoria recounted that as a young father Buck "kept a number of braided green switches, made of willow and walnut twigs, and with these stinging weapons, never with an ordinary whip, he would cut the quivering flesh of his children till their tears and blood melted him into mercy."[5] Victoria's mother was only marginally better. Roxy was a religious fanatic who quickly realized that spiritual enthusiasm could be monetized in a society that had lost its way. She also had a vague inkling that spiritualism—and being possessed by spirits, benign or maleficent—could give a woman authority in a culture that intended to render her powerless. Women like Roxy and her daughters, Victoria and Tennessee, were regularly silenced in the public sphere of their time. But when they spoke as spiritualists, for God, or ghosts, or demons, these women suddenly drew immense audiences. As Victoria would later write: "Do not, however, receive this as coming from me; but accept it as coming from the wisest and best of ascended Spirits—those whom you have learned to honor and love for the good done while on the earthly plane." Roxy Claflin encouraged her daughters to converse with the here-beyond, to listen for otherworldly voices, but more importantly, to prophesize, to speak for spirits. This was a wise parental choice, maybe the only one: in the wake of the Civil War, as a nation of mourners tried to communicate with spirits loved and lost, these skills became lucrative.

At fifteen, however, Victoria, who later made her name as a clairvoyant, had no inkling of her future fortune. She was a sickly teenager, "ignorant, innocent, and simple," who, on the Fourth of July 1853, met a handsomely bearded doctor named Canning Woodhull.[6] Woodhull took to the girl immediately: "Puss," he said, "tell your father and mother I want you for a wife."[7] Even at the time, the command must have sounded slightly off-putting, but Victoria immediately acquiesced: any home was better than the one she had with her father. Unfortunately, unbeknownst to his new bride, Canning drank more heavily than Buck, and his hands were only slightly more tethered. The couple moved almost immediately to Chicago. Victoria was pregnant with a son, Byron, who was born in a low frame house, in a frigid room, with physical and mental impediments that Victoria quietly attributed to her husband's perpetual drunkenness. For a moment, Victoria appeared trapped. But only for a moment. She moved her family to San Francisco, and began a lifelong project of reinvention, first as a cigar salesgirl, then as a seamstress, and finally an actress. Acting was not a stretch for the girl who had, at the age of twelve, insisted to her mother that she communed with angels.

Victoria was a success onstage, earning more than fifty dollars a week (a seamstress would earn five), and single-handedly placed her family on stable, if temporary, financial footing. Her marriage to the carousing Canning Woodhull, however, was in shambles. In the coming year, Victoria, who had no doubt reconsidered the relative merits of her marital choice, returned east to her family of origin. By then Buck and Roxy Claflin had launched a profitable family business: a traveling roadshow of mystics, healers, and crystal-ball readers. Victoria joined the caravan in a heartbeat, sweeping through the small farming communities of Ohio and Indiana, curing townspeople of all manner of affliction. She specialized as a medical healer in the "laying on of hands," which supposedly galvanized the energies of her patients, but also as a fortune teller who helped clients negotiate their future and come to terms with their past. Undoubtedly, most of Victoria's methods were fraudulent—which is to say too wild for belief—but such methods have been taken seriously with surprising frequency in American history. Victoria came to make an utter fortune from her wildness.

WHEN VICTORIA MET James Blood in 1864, it was the star-crossing of two spiritualists, individuals whose metaphysical beliefs—their common understanding of God, the soul, death, and the afterlife—were translated into a shared life of love and freedom. This sounds more pious than it ever was. Most women who were "clairvoyants" and "healers" were also regularly regarded, and maligned, as prostitutes. It wasn't always clear exactly what the "laying on of hands" meant in healing spaces like Victoria's. She later reflected that her untraditional courtship with James transpired "by way of the air"—a reference to ghostly transmissions—but much more might have been involved. Really, it doesn't matter. James and Victoria were on the same path to "free love," a radical position in the postwar era, which held that passionate conviction and spiritual connection should trump any and all conventional social arrangements, including monogamy and traditional marriage. When Victoria prophesized that they would be husband and wife, James was one of the few already married men in America who would have, on principle, been open to the suggestion—as he was.[8]

James, a tall, fine-looking man edging thirty, had married his first wife as many people do: out of habit and prudence. At the beginning of the Civil War, Blood served as St. Louis city auditor and lived a life by the book: conservative, increasingly wealthy, in a stark white house with his two daughters and wife. But then Blood experienced the atrocities of Bloody Kansas and watched his native Missouri ripped apart by warring factions over the issue of slavery. His own body had been riddled by bullets in four separate battles, including one of the bloodiest of the war at Vicksburg. When he was discharged from the army early in 1864, he assumed a position in St. Louis that would very slowly, but steadily, lead him away from respectability.

James became the head of the St. Louis Spiritualist Society, an organization whose members claimed to converse with wraiths and specters. For Blood's part, he was said to regularly commune with his fallen comrades. The St. Louis spiritualists were not, at this particular juncture, a fringe population, but rather a group that was gaining sway in American society. They were remarkably philosophical about their social and romantic relationships and reflected an idealism in a society in need of hope. True freedom was not realized in political or military triumphs but rather in the subjective feeling—individual, all-encompassing, absolute—of profound liberty and belonging. The consonance with earlier American Bloods, like Thaddeus and Perez, could not be clearer: nationwide movements in the name of freedom often missed the point of wildness. James and Victoria, in their singular union, would not.

Mere days after their initial meeting in St. Louis—in a mystical union, as Woodhull described it, consummated "on the spot by the powers of air"—the couple eloped. Colonel Blood left his wife, daughters, good name, and a debt of $3,700 behind. Seemingly advised by a woman who knew the business, he purchased a brightly colored wagon with a grand canopy, and the lovers set off through the Ozarks as traveling healers and fortune tellers under the name of "Dr. and Mrs. James Harvey."[9] Victoria was a natural: "healing" customers with a mixture of homegrown medicine, folk wisdom, compassion, blind faith, and animal magnetism. Blood served as the manager of the operation and slowly saved enough money to pay his debts. He returned to St. Louis long enough to do so, and then they were off again to Chicago, to join the Claflin family in their Wabash Avenue home, which was about to become a house of ill repute.[10]

The accusations of prostitution and blackmail that had always swirled around Buck Claflin finally landed. He had spent the better part of his adult life coercing his daughters and visiting servant girls into entertaining male guests and then, according to Victoria, turning around to blackmail these guests by pretending to be the father of several ruined virgins. The landlord on Wabash canceled the house's lease and evicted the family. Tennessee, whose wit and beauty rivaled Victoria's, found refuge with her older sister and Colonel Blood, and the trio made at least a tacit agreement to sideline Roxy and Buck in any future business dealings. For the first time, Victoria and Tennessee, under the guardianship of James Blood, could think for themselves, and that is exactly what they did. Ultimately, they wouldn't need his protection, either.

SO DID BLOOD and Woodhull ever get married and live happily ever after? No. Yes. Well—it's complicated. As mentioned before, in the 1850s, the American Midwest was a borderland, the place where the United States as a functioning nation-state reached its limits. A decade later, St. Louis became the intellectual outpost for thinkers to reconceive the meaning and value of liberty, in matters both political and domestic. Situated on the verge of a no-man's-land, the westernmost edge of civilization, the city attracted thinkers like Blood who were drawn to intellectual frontiers—to radical socialism, feminism, anarchism, and philosophical idealism. When he first met Victoria, Blood was already well versed in the philosophy that would come to guide their careers. His American strain of spiritualism drew inspiration from two European sources: the utopian vision of Charles Fourier and the mysticism of Emanuel Swedenborg.

Fourier, who is credited with coining the term "feminism" in 1837, held that cooperation between equals, divorced from systems of modern capital, could be the basis of a lasting utopia, and that the oppression of women in the early nineteenth century (their lack of suffrage, social status, and economic mobility) stood as the principal impediment to truly progressive ideals. In his first book-length treatment of the subject, *Théorie des quatre mouvements et des destinées générales*, published anonymously in 1808, Fourier explained:

> Is not a young woman a piece of merchandise put up for
> sale to the highest bidder? Is not the consent that she gives

to marriage derisory and forced on her by the lifelong tyranny of prejudice? People try to persuade her that she is only bound by chains of flowers. But can she really doubt her degradation, even in nations that are puffed up with philosophy like England? . . . It is known that the best nations have always been those which concede the greatest amount of liberty to women. This is true of the barbarians and the savages as well as of the civilized . . . As a general proposition: Social progress and changes of period are brought about by virtue of the progress of women toward liberty, and social retrogression occurs as a result of a diminution in the liberty of women. Other events influence these political changes; but there is no cause which produces social progress or decline as rapidly as a change in the condition of women.[11]

Victoria Woodhull

"In sum, the extension of women's rights," Fourier concluded, "is the basic principle of all social progress."[12] Fourier suggested that traditional marriage, and therefore contemporary love, hamstrung the possibilities of women, and argued for something like Goethe's "elective affinities," that could wax and wane and pass out of existence as a couple saw fit.

This probably suited Blood and Woodhull, and their previous partners not at all. As soon as their spirits met, there was absolutely no power that could tear them asunder. They were divorced—at least in their own minds—before any court or church proceedings could run their course. In fact, when James and Victoria were *first* married in 1865, at least the groom was still married to his first wife, Mary. James: the free-loving, spiritual Blood bigamist. But that's how it is. At the time, the punishment for bigamy was a five-hundred-dollar fine and two years in jail. When Blood moved with his lover back to Chicago, where moral and legal standards were a bit more lax, they had the opportunity to marry again. At last, in 1866, Mary Blood filed for divorce with just cause—adultery—and James was free to marry whomever he chose. He was already with Victoria, but now he was officially ready to bolt with his new wife and her sister to New York.

From the outside, the newlyweds' behavior seemed erratic and impetuous, but from the inside, from the perspective of two lovers, switchbacks and U-turns are almost always interpreted as a matter of fate, or better yet, divine providence. American spiritualists like James and Victoria took their cues from Fourier, but increasingly from the teachings of Emanuel Swedenborg, the Swedish eighteenth-century mystic and seer whose uncanny revelations bewitched a generation of American and

European thinkers. At first, Swedenborg's visions appeared only in dreams, symbolic scenes to be interpreted with care. But one evening in 1745, Swedenborg's premonitions enveloped his waking hours. As he ate in a local tavern, he suddenly became aware of a swamp teeming with life, encroaching on his dining table. In the corner of the tavern, an unknown gentleman materialized who admonished him not to succumb to gluttony, followed him home, announced that he was Jesus Christ, and finally announced that humanity stood in need of a definitive Bible lesson and Swedenborg had been selected to provide it. And if that wasn't enough, Jesus said that Emanuel could visit the spirit realm whenever he chose. Swedenborg's account of the afterlife, experienced personally and immediately and set down in *Introducing the New Jerusalem*, placed modern Christianity on a new and radical footing. "Heaven is not located on high," Swedenborg stated, flirting with heresy, "but where the good of love is, and this resides in a person, wherever he or she is."[13] And so the religious and philosophical ground of the "free love" movement was prepared.

Crucial for James and Victoria, Swedenborg had claimed not only direct access to God and the heavens but also to the future, predicting calamities near and far, from the death of the emperor of Russia to the destruction of a small mill in his hometown. Swedenborg would never broadcast, much less market, his psychic powers, but this didn't keep many of his American followers, like James and Victoria, from doing precisely that. Their legal troubles temporarily behind them, the couple joined Tennessee and took up residence at 17 Great Jones Street, nestled in the throbbing heart of New York City, between present-day SoHo and the East Village. The Claflin sisters were perfectly at home in this neighborhood of peddlers, gamblers, and drunks, but they gravitated to the stockbrokers who strode downtown through the Village each morning.[14] Blood and the sisters made their living as fortune tellers, but to a growing number of financiers they became investment advisors. Every evening, at eleven o'clock, James Blood welcomed a faithful audience into his home on Great Jones Street. The lights were dimmed, the crowd was seated, and Victoria took center stage. Falling into a trance, apparently possessed by ghostly voices, she held forth on topics that ranged from the destiny of women's rights to the fluctuating prices of commodities. It may seem far-fetched, but genuinely powerful men came to rely on her preternatural foresight, none more so than the American shipping and railroad magnate Cornelius Vanderbilt.

Vanderbilt was recently widowed and in the twilight of his life when he crossed paths with Blood and the psychic sisters. He immediately fell in love with Tennessee and remained in awe of Victoria. Victoria had a knack for what today is termed "insider trading"; she invited wealthy businessmen into her séances, pumped them for information about their respective professions, and used this information to advise other clients on future investments. In September 1869, she began to guide Vanderbilt in his buying and selling of gold. When the dust cleared on the Black Friday of September 24 (a day that witnessed gold prices devalued by 20 percent in a matter of minutes), Vanderbilt emerged 1.3 million dollars richer, thanks solely to Victoria.[15] Legend has it that Victoria Claflin Woodhull Blood herself made seven hundred thousand dollars that month, but whatever the exact figure, it was enough to vault the family into the national spotlight and, very quickly, into the middle of New York's stockbroking realm. With James Blood as the figurehead and Vanderbilt as backer, Victoria launched the first woman-centered brokerage in history. They set up shop in the exclusive Hoffman House at 44 Broad Street, and when they opened their doors on the fourteenth of February 1870, one hundred policemen had to hold back the crowd. The brokerage was geared to the wealthy women of Manhattan, an untapped market in the financial sector, and the "bewitching brokers," as *Harper's Magazine* described them, cornered it completely.[16]

WHERE WAS JAMES BLOOD in all of this? It is at once a very good and completely irrelevant question. The fact is that Blood had married a force of nature, so it really doesn't matter where he was situated in the rising tide that would carry Victoria Woodhull into the public eye. But it should be said that Blood would have never placed his bets with such a woman were it not for his extremely liberal political convictions, which he voiced routinely—through her.

After forming the brokerage, James, Victoria, and Tennessee founded *Woodhull and Claflin's Weekly* in May 1870, the principal organ of radical free thinking in America in the second half of the nineteenth century. The newspaper's slogan—"PROGRESS! FREE THOUGHT! UNTRAMMELLED LIVES! BREAKING THE WAY FOR FUTURE GENERATIONS"—said it all and resonated deeply with women suffragists in the Northeast and across the country.[17] Most of the articles of the newly formed paper were written by Blood and fellow spiritualist-anarchist Stephen Pearl Andrews.

The *Weekly* accomplished great things in the early 1870s, among them publishing the first English translation of Marx's *Communist Manifesto* in the United States and providing a platform for Woodhull's groundbreaking run at the presidency, as the country's first female candidate.

In a rare practically oriented suggestion, James Blood urged his wife to ally herself closely to the less radical suffragists, Susan B. Anthony and Elizabeth Cady Stanton, and supported her when she announced a controversial running mate: Frederick Douglass (although Douglass was never notified, and never acknowledged the nomination, for fear of being closely associated with Victoria's radical libertarianism). The ticket of Woodhull's Equal Rights Party didn't stand a chance, but the point was not necessarily to win, it was to demonstrate a bold possibility, explored on the basis of uncompromising principles. It was not only a chance to capture the limelight, but also to highlight aspects of the American political system that had remained in shadow. And why not? This too was an aspect of realizing happiness in America. Being an American Blood meant pursuing the unachievable, even and perhaps especially beyond the bounds of sound judgment. At the very least, there was no confusion about who was responsible when things went wildly awry.

By some accounts, it was James Harvey Blood, Woodhull's loyal companion, who led her into a radical life and, ultimately, the public eye. For while he was a spiritualist, James was also an advocate for free love and fiat money (the idea that currency didn't have to be backed by anything). Many writers of his day tried to come to terms with his various beliefs, rendering a picture of a man who was half anarchist, half socialist, and 100 percent mystic. These were the ideals at the core of his relationship with Woodhull, who would graft them onto her fervent call for women's suffrage.

The Civil War had created a space for Woodhull and Blood—an openness to alternative ways of social and political life. The war had also created the existential impetus for many people to deviate from conventions and roles that had structured antebellum America. Calamity has its uses—it can motivate a people to seek happiness in different places while there is still time. In the midst of her first presidential race (she ran again, if half-heartedly, in 1879 and 1892), Woodhull stood on the floor of Congress and said something that Blood women of the past surely had longed to say: "I come before you to declare that my sex are entitled to the inalienable right to life, liberty, and the pursuit of happiness."[18] Victoria would not win a single electoral vote.

And here is where the already fascinating story of James Harvey Blood and Victoria Woodhull (Blood) becomes genuinely wild. These Bloods believed, among other things, in reincarnation, and it is possible to read the turn of events that defined James's later life against the backdrop of his family history and, particularly, the Bloods' occasional treatment—or mistreatment—of women. One story from Blood family lore frames James and Victoria's fate in an almost preternatural way: this is the tale of Elvira Blood.

Elvira was the whip-thin wife of Capt. Samuel Blood, a seafarer with a home port on the central coast of Maine. In the 1830s, Samuel spent most of his time on dry land at the Mariner's Club, eating and drinking away the family's livelihood. Elvira did not look kindly on Sam's behavior. One night, an

especially nice dinner was served at the Club, but before the patrons could eat the meal, the table was upset by a cloaked man
who darted out of the tavern. Sam and his friends gave chase
and finally caught the meal-wrecker. It turned out to be not a
man at all, but rather an exasperated Elvira Blood.[19] Today,
such a demonstration of female autonomy would be expected if
not applauded, but not in Sam's day. As punishment for the em-
barrassment, Sam decided to take Elvira to sea with him—to
South America. Upon nearing the equator, his American crew
decided that they had gone far enough and shipped back to
the United States, reporting that the trip had not been particularly kind to the wife of Captain Blood. Even so, Sam and
Elvira carried on with a skeleton crew. When Sam eventually
returned home the following year, he was alone. He somberly
reported that Elvira had died of unknown causes off the coast
of Jamaica. But most of the townspeople suspected she died of
unnatural causes. Sam was banned from the Mariner's Club for
a reason that only a fellow spiritualist could appreciate: every
time he came to dinner, his table was mysteriously overturned,
all the food and drink, dishes and utensils, crashing to the

Victoria
Woodhull
before the
Senate
committee

floor. It didn't matter what precautions were taken, the meal never got to be eaten.

Turning back to James Harvey Blood and Victoria Woodhull, one might read the breakup of these two spiritual seekers (and James's eventual demise) as the ultimate form of Elvira's revenge. Upon losing the presidential election of 1872 to Ulysses S. Grant and being imprisoned for circulating obscene literature about her critics in her newspaper, Woodhull decided that she was not cut out to be a radical after all. And she essentially pitched James Blood overboard—divorcing him on fabricated grounds of adultery in the winter of 1875.[20] The *Weekly* closed in more or less disrepute in 1876. In January 1877, Woodhull's benefactor Cornelius Vanderbilt died, with an estimated fortune of $110 million. In the legal struggle for the money, Woodhull managed to squeeze a small fortune out of the family, enough to buy a snug house at 8 Gilston Road, Southampton, England. And enough for her and her sister to uphold at least the appearance of respectable English gentlewomen.

Victoria may have no longer been a Blood in any legal sense, but she still acted like one, freeing herself from her past in order to secure a more a fruitful, if not necessarily more liberating, future. Survival was all that mattered, and to this end she had to be rid of the good colonel and his radical ideas. She wrote in the conservative *Humanitarian*: "During no part of my life did I favor Free Love even tacitly . . . I regarded it with loathing when once I got a slight idea of its character and the deep infamy to which it led."[21] She protested: the most radical articles in the *Weekly* had been written by her husband of the time, Mr. Blood, without her knowledge or permission. This just-so story, one that cut the colonel out of Victoria's life, was managed and amplified for exactly one reason: to secure a more respectable husband, whom she found in John Martin, an English banker more suited to her new, more traditional persona. It took Victoria another seven years to convince the Martin family that she was respectable enough to marry him in 1883.

When Victoria jettisoned James Blood, he fled to the central coast of Maine. He turned gaunt and even more eccentric, supposedly eating two cups of raw wheat a day. Ashamed of his clothes and physical appearance, he'd walk the streets of town only at night. He, unlike Victoria, remained true to his belief in free love and offered his services as a "spiritual healer." And he took up sailing. He didn't malign Woodhull, only stating that the "greatest woman in the world" had let him go.

In fact, many of his neighbors believed that Blood never gave up hope of winning Victoria back by striking it rich. Blood eventually secured a clerkship on Governors Island, the 172-acre island in New York Harbor, then tried his hand at running a refreshment shop on Coney Island, at last returning to his spiritual ways as a carnival exhibitionist of mesmerism. One day he was visited by an African seer who told him he was destined to find a gold mine in West Africa. So he left on an 1885 voyage to the Ivory Coast in search of treasure. He found what he was looking for, yet he never saw Victoria again. A vial of gold accompanied Blood's body when it was shipped back to Brooklyn in 1886. The villagers outside Accra, on the coast of present-day Ghana, said that he died under mysterious circumstances involving "black medicine."[22]

"Black medicine" indeed. All of this could be something like "Elvira's revenge" on the cult of masculinity that held sway for the American Bloods. Victoria Woodhull, unlike Elvira Blood, lived on quite happily into old age, founding a more respectable newspaper in London that was truly her own, spending her considerable fortune restoring George Washington's estate in England (she somehow claimed to be related to the president), and securing the standing and success that women of previous generations could not have envisioned. In the history of the American Bloods, Victoria acted the part: to do as a matter of course what others could hardly condone and scarcely imagine.

THE MYSTIC ≡≡≡

I saw a moving sight the other morning before breakfast in a little hotel where I slept in the dusty fields. The young man of the house shot a little wolf called coyote in the early morning. The little heroic animal lay on the ground, with his big furry ears, and his clean white teeth, and his little cheerful body, but his little brave life was gone. It made me think how brave all living things are.

—WILLIAM JAMES
TO HIS SON, ALEXANDER, 1898[1]

A "LITTLE WOLF"—TRICKSTER, TEACHER, KEEPER of magic, brave one, wild thing—is almost always larger than life. In the passing of years, I have come to believe that the creature of Wolf Rock, on the edge of Blood Farm, was just this sort of beast. It chased me through the Tophet Swamp, past its ancestral home, back to my own, where I discovered the American Bloods, a clan of inexplicable and untamed beasts, who, even in their failings and ultimate demise, make me think "how brave all living things are."

IN 1837, HAVING interviewed the minuteman Thaddeus Blood, Ralph Waldo Emerson wrote the "Concord Hymn," an account of the "shot heard round the world" at the outset of a battle for unbroken freedom. Two decades later, Henry David Thoreau, inspired by Perez Blood, fashioned his own more expansive philosophy of wilderness: "All good things," he wrote, "are wild and free." Why? Because, as he explains: "We need the tonic of wildness . . . At the same time that we are earnest to explore and learn all things, we require that all things be mysterious and unexplorable, that land and sea be indefinitely wild, unsurveyed and unfathomed by us because unfathomable."[2] Emerson and Thoreau were always, and rightfully, concerned that the industry and convention of "normal life" would level the possibilities and idiosyncrasies of being human, that wildness would somehow be fully tamed.

If there is a single American thinker who inherited the transcendentalism of Emerson and Thoreau—and its insistence that the point of living was to chart one's own way—it is William James. This "adorable genius," as he was called by his friend Oliver Wendell Holmes, was a polymath of unparalleled proportions. He became a painter, teacher, biologist, chemist, psychologist, philosopher, theologian, mystic, and hiker—all of the first degree. There is still a joke that circulates through Boston and Harvard Square that between William James and his novelist brother Henry, William was the superior writer. There might be something to it. In the course of his long career at Harvard, James would found the discipline of empirical psychology and a genuinely American school of philosophy, what came to be known as pragmatism, that attempted to wed the practical and empirical to the spiritual and transcendent. William James is, for many people, the quintessential American scholar. He is, at least for me.

James, however, was no god, and is all the more appealing because of his deep humanity—his fallibility and vulnerability. That being said, he came from one of the wealthiest families in the state of New York, and his grandfather William practically owned the city of Albany. The James children never had to work. They had only one job: to be as free as humanly possible. Easier said than done. James's friend Richard Cabot once commented that being born into great wealth meant that a child had to succeed beyond all bounds or entirely fail, and I think

William James   Benjamin Paul Blood

this is the case for young William. He was encouraged to seize every opportunity, and this strange pressure had an adverse effect on his psyche. He spent his twenties and thirties aimless and suicidally depressed. Before he made a name in the Ivy League as Harvard's chosen son, he wanted nothing to do with academic life. During this time, he found academic life constricting and bloodless, and turned to any compelling teacher who was willing to take him to the outer reaches of life and consciousness. It should come as no surprise that he found an enduring guide in a seer-mystic named Benjamin Paul Blood.

Born in 1832 in Amsterdam, New York, ten miles to the northwest of James's native Albany, Benjamin Blood would be described in various ways: as "a bardic poet," "a fancy gymnast," "a pugilist," "a psychedelic philosopher," "an eccentric inventor," "a successful gambler." And "a mad one."[3] But according to the fathers of American philosophy, he was mad in just the right way. In December 1854, Emerson wrote to his cousin William: "A Mr. Blood of New York has written a good poem called 'Bride of the Iconoclast.'"[4] This young "Mr. Blood" was Benjamin, a man akin to the "little wolf" of Wolf Rock—a beast that belonged to another age, or a mythological creature belonging to no age at all, or a reminder that the unfathomable loves to hide.

Benjamin was just twenty-two years old when he anonymously published *The Bride of the Iconoclast*, a hundred-page poem consisting of five Spenserian cantos and reflecting the most essential transcendentalist intuition that, as Thoreau puts it, "in wildness is the preservation of the world." The poem recounts the star-crossed love of the "iconoclast," Barron, and his beloved, Hermia. When the poem opens, Barron is living where an increasing number of Americans lived: in a dull, stultifying city where nothing ever happens. But then Hermia enters the scene and things change dramatically: they fall in love, and everyday life, the tired trappings of civilization, falls away. They become, in the poet's words, "large-souled and calm, true nature worshippers."[5]

In the introduction to the poem, Blood instructs his reader that it is to be read on "grim hills [that] bristle with sunshine . . . where truth dwells in nature's nakedness rough hewn and wild."[6] Only in such a spot could one understand the sublime experience of Barron and Hermia, or the tragedy that befalls them. In the third canto, pirates kidnap Hermia, and she drowns before Barron can save her. The pirates also vanish in a storm at sea, and Barron, in his solitude, offers the reader a final warning: "Be brave, for thou art watching thee; be kind / Thou ever shall keep company thyself." Emerson was in total agreement with the young Blood. "Whoso would be a man," he wrote, "must be a nonconformist" or, in Blood's words, "an iconoclast." To turn away from society, to turn toward nature, to turn into oneself—this was a rare act of bravery. The danger was real, but so too was the reward—the experience, vivid yet fleeting, of Barron and Hermia, who "stood up alone in that wide universe" in "a soft dawning light . . . warm, red, and sultry."[7] Today, there are two of Blood's writings that remain in Emerson's library, held at the Concord Museum and Harvard's Houghton Library. One is *The Bride of the Iconoclast*, which described a mystical frontier, the outlying possibilities of being human. The other is a thirty-seven-page pamphlet titled *The Anaesthetic Revelation and the Gist of Philosophy*, published in 1874, which charted a course toward that very border. And it is this *Revelation* that caught the attention of Emerson's intellectual godson, William James, in the fall of 1874.

BENJAMIN, LIKE HIS forebearers, explored a frontier, but in this case it was the uncharted borderlands not of a young and fragile nation but of the human mind, supple and expansive. In his thirties, with the help of psychotropics, he tested a hypothesis that the American Bloods had always explored: that a man or woman only discovers themselves at the limits of reality, in an act of transcendence. "After experiments ranging nearly fourteen years," he wrote, "I affirm what any man may prove at will, that there is an invariable and reliable condition (or uncondition) ensuing about the instant of recall from anaesthetic stupor to sensible observation, or 'coming to,' IN WHICH THE GENIUS OF BEING IS REVEALED." This might have been the first detailed account of a psychedelic trip in the United States, but Blood is clear that it is also the description of "coming to" or arriving at a vista overlooking uncharted territories. This enduring sense of "more," of heedlessness that stretches out without end, captured William James's attention and forever altered the course of his intellectual life. James wrote of *The Anaesthetic Revelation*: "I forget how it fell into my hands, but it fascinated me so 'weirdly' that I am conscious of its having been one of the stepping-stones of my thinking ever since."[8]

James knew there was a type of madness in his friend Blood, a freedom that stood to alienate his staid New England neighbors, men and women who had largely forgotten their own untamed origins. James counseled patience, writing, "Now, although we are more than skeptical of the importance of Mr. Blood's so-called discovery, we shall not howl with the wolves or join the multitude in jeering at it. Nirwana, whether called by that name or not, has been conceived and represented as the consummation of life too often not to have some meaning."[9] Nirvana, according to Benjamin Blood, was not an idea to be considered but a reality, a mystery, to be experienced. James regarded this position as a practical invitation, spending the better part of a decade testing near-fatal doses of nitrous oxide in search of Blood's mind-blowing reality.

I never really understood James's friendship with Benjamin until I met the rest of the American Bloods. I was just too much of a philosopher—too much in my head, not firmly enough tethered to the world. Blood, like James, harbored a not-so-quiet suspicion of philosophy. It isn't that philosophy is worthless, but rather that it always feigns to accomplish more, much more, than it can ever deliver. Philosophy aims to give the last word on life and its meaning, but in truth it has the unfortunate tendency to theorize life to death. Any irregularity, any excess, any uncanny aspect of reality, is shaved off by its intellectual scalpel. The simpler, the better. Its theories, pristine and clean, abstract and ideal, have little to do with the subterranean forces that animate human nature. Historically, philosophers have overlooked and therefore discounted the wild—which is to say euphoric and horrific—realizations of men like Benjamin Blood.

The most important insight philosophy can offer is an honest statement of its own limitations and inadequacy, or as Blood wrote in his *Revelation*, "The gist of all philosophy [is its] own insufficiency to comprehend or in any way state the All."[10] Blood's mystical "All" is not to be honored in a traditional religious ceremony, or described exhaustively by the intellect, but rather felt in the simple acknowledgment that life, in the words of Walt Whitman, contains multitudes—space for contradictions and tensions and paradoxes that we feel yet cannot fully understand. Summarizing Blood's insight, William James explains that "the secret of Being, in short, is not the dark immensity *beyond* knowledge, but at home, this side, beneath the feet, and *overlooked* by knowledge."[11] Blood and James begin to give form to sentiments expressed repeatedly by Thoreau, realized on his evening walks across the hills of Blood Farm: "Heaven is under our feet as well as above our heads."[12] It is not that heaven or absolute freedom eludes us but rather that we elude it—like the undeniable, unmistakable wildness that lingers in our backyard.

According to Benjamin Blood, most of us discount any experience that might fall outside the narrow confines of normalcy, to our own detriment. Nearly two hundred years before Michael Pollan suggested that psychedelics could "change your mind," Benjamin was on to the twofold meaning of the suggestion. Psychedelics alter one's consciousness in order to "let more in," to open up and air out the tiny skull-sized kingdoms that we call our "minds." Life is richer than you think. Reality is stranger than you might believe—and far, far stranger than you could ever put to words. And freedom is wilder than you ever expect. In Blood's words, the central "point of illumination," a point that lasts long after the psychedelic vision has faded, is this:

That sanity is not the basic quality of intelligence, but rather a mere condition which is variable and like the humming of a wheel goes up or down the musical gamut according to physical activity . . . but life in its nakedness

is realized only outside of sanity altogether . . . and that
the awful Mystery of life is now but a homely and common
thing.[13]

If this doesn't make perfect sense, perhaps a bit of forbear-
ance is warranted. James admitted to Blood: "Your thought
is obscure,—lightning flashes, darting gleams—but that is the
way the truth is."[14] When Blood wrote to Alfred, Lord Tennyson inquiring whether the great poet had experienced such a
revelation, Tennyson responded in a note (published in *The New
York Times* on December 6, 1874) that he had never taken drugs
to induce such a state but had experienced these trances since
boyhood and they were "beyond words."[15] That is, after all, the
point of the Anesthetic Revelation: it reveals, beyond doubt, a
reality that escapes perfect comprehension. And this reality,
far from being some otherworldly realm, is our reality, all the
time—like the coyotes in the woods that are always there but
almost always unseen. For those who have caught a glimpse, it
provides a sort of lasting revision of mind, one that can trans-
form one's life from within. Tennyson remarked to Blood "that
when I return to my moral state of sanity I am ready to fight for
'*Meine Liebes Ich*,' and hold that it will last for aeons and aeons."[16]

Meine Liebes Ich: "My dear I"—the transcendental vision
somehow remains close, heartfelt, grounding, while at the
same time mysterious, wondrous, and sublime. The "secret of
Being" was, for Blood, revealed in the deceptively simple act
of "coming to." In one sense, discovery is a matter of venturing elsewhere and taking a trip, but in another, it is the act of
waking up to what is inevitably present. It is sometimes the
experience of stumbling onto something else, just beyond the

scope of one's present attention, the feeling of "coming to": coming to consciousness, coming to a New World, coming to a place, strange, slippery, but immediately present. Blood's was a distinctive mysticism, pluralistic rather than monistic in its focus, dynamic rather than static in its form. James, who was drawn to the mystical insight, but who eschewed the belief in some transcendent (read "controlling") Absolute, was hooked.

IN THE ENSUING decades, Benjamin Blood and William James were regular correspondents. In a note dated June 11, 1887, Benjamin wrote: "I have no picture, alas, save to send you the one that I enclose, taken for devilment some fifteen years ago . . . when I had lifted by a chain over my right shoulder and around my right arm a weight of 1160 pounds. You will say of it with Virgil, '*Arma virumque.*'" As in "*Arma virumque cano*"—the first line of the *Aeneid*—"I sing of arms and the man."[17] William James would sing, and he wouldn't be alone: Emerson along with Tennyson and Robert Louis Stevenson would join the chorus in praise of Blood.

The portrait that Blood sent to James is an image of a singular human being—square jaw, black eyes, Nietzschean mustache, rolled short sleeves, bow tie—ready to lift an unreasonable weight. Upon receiving the photograph, James wrote to Blood: "I confess, that I did not expect the author of your works to look just like that, and am anxious to see the later editions of the creature . . . I am so delighted to find that a metaphysician can be anything else than a . . . dyspeptic individual fit for no use. Most of them have been invalids."[18] Benjamin most certainly was not an invalid; James confirmed his robustness in an 1895 visit to Amsterdam. Self-descriptions are seldom objectively accurate, but they have the uncanny ability to reveal something essential of their author. After the meeting, Blood wrote to James:

> I was born here in Amsterdam. My father was a land holder of 700 acres [2.8 km²] here, adjoining the city on both sides of the river, and lived, as I now live, in a large brick house on the south bank of the Mohawk visible as you enter Amsterdam from the east. I was his only child, and went a good deal my own way. I ran to machinery, by fancy; patented among other devices a swathing reaper which is very successful. I was of loose and wandering ways. And was a successful gambler through the Tweed regime—made 'bar'ls' of money, and threw it away. I was a fancy gymnast also, and have had some heavy fights, notable one of forty minutes with Ed. Mullett, whom I left senseless. This was mere fancy. I never lifted an angry hand against man, woman or child—all fun—for me . . . I do farming in a way, but am much idle. I have been a sort of pet of the city, and think I should be missed. In a large vote taken by one of the daily papers here a month or so ago as to who were the 12 leading citizens, I was 6th in the 12, and sole in my class. So you see, if Sparta has many a worthier son, I am still boss in the department I prefer. It may seem foolish—supererogatory—to say all this, yet I think it otherwise. It were different with you people who are known hereditarily . . . I could never value things at others' rates—never was respectable or conforming; but truth and honesty are a fashion by themselves, and I have lived to my ways, once called heterodox, now merely

advanced; the chaff blows off, the grain remains and I
would borrow the city's treasure if I wanted the money—
which (I sometimes think, unfortunately) I never did.[19]

Today Blood is known, if he is known at all, for his philosophy and experimental drug use, but his intellectual pursuits
should be regarded, I think, as an afterthought to action, the
trace of a life lived as fully as possible. Benjamin's philosophy—
which he kept developing over almost seven decades, starting in
the early 1850s—put to paper what the American Bloods had,
over three centuries, come to know by heart: "Not unfortunately, the universe is wild—game flavored as a hawk's wing,"[20]
Blood wrote. "Nature is miracle all. She knows no laws; the
same returns not, save to bring the different. The slow round
of the engraver's lathe gains but the breadth of a hair, but the
difference is distributed back over the whole curve, never an
instant true—ever not quite."[21]

James was drawn to the promise of a wild universe, to the
idea that there was always something yet to be explored, a re-
mainder that could not be tabulated, an unknown animal that
would never be seen again. Our understanding of reality will
forever be, in Blood's words, "ever not quite." And this is "not
unfortunate." At the beginning of the twentieth century, philosophers worried that the hope of radical freedom and origi-
nality, the hope of a country born into Thoreau's wildness, was
beginning, ever so slowly, to fade. And with it, the prospects of
a meaningful life. If things were too well-ordered, too united,
there would be no wiggle room for freedom. Blood and James
could not abide the threat. In 1896, James sent Blood a small
pamphlet titled "Is Life Worth Living?," an essay that would
be a cornerstone of *The Will to Believe* and James's mature

philosophy. In short, the answer is maybe. Maybe life is worth living; in James's words, "it depends on the liver."

There are no guarantees or safety nets to secure life's worth. The task of life may be to live thoughtfully, but never to sacrifice life and its precious "maybes" for the sake of pure contemplation. We are never to shirk the consequences of our precarious choices and circumstances. When Blood and James had met in Amsterdam the year before, they sat at Benjamin's table and debated the meaning of life, at which point Blood confided again to James that he found little in philosophy itself to excite or enliven him. "I felt compelled to go into more active life," he admitted, "and since then I have been in our mills ten hours a day, missing only a day or two. I am at 'condition' pitch and the weeks fly by unheeded, and life is worth living."

The American Bloods conversed with and influenced the greatest thinkers of their day, but they chose to prioritize action over mere thought—a risky and morally complex choice that is open to us all. What is it to live in "condition" pitch other than this? In a letter to Blood written in June 1896, James echoes his friend: "Fear of life in one form or other is the great thing to exorcise; but it isn't reason that will ever do it. Impulse without reason is enough, and reason without impulse is a poor make-shift. I take it that no man is ever educated who has never dallied with that thought of suicide." The American Bloods, with stunning consistency, came to close quarters with the "fear of life," and in many cases, and with varying results, managed to exorcise it by living on the brink.

"Variety, not uniformity," Benjamin would later write, "is more likely to be the key to progress. The genius of being is whimsical rather than consistent. Our strata show broken bones of histories all forgotten. How can it be otherwise? There

can be no purpose of eternity. It is process all. The most sublime result, if it appeared as the ultimatum, would go stale in
an hour; it could not be endured."[22] Benjamin Blood's mystical
insights—his understanding of what is real and what is not—
inspired the pluralism of his and James's later philosophical life.
Looking back on his friend's poetry, an aged James admitted
to Blood: "How I wish that I too could write poetry, for pluralism is in its *Sturm und Drang* period, and verse is the only way to
express certain things."[23] As American life homogenized and
flattened, Benjamin's ideas articulated a vibrant "pluraliverse,"
a reality that could not be reduced to a static whole but rather
a diversity of paths that coursed through the field of possibility,
trails that one could explore at his or her own risk and reward.
"I am a pluralist easily enough," he wrote to James in 1897,
"believing only in low-case gods, and in no grand climactic results of being; there is no finale, no one lesson to be learned . . .
all days are judgment-days and creation-morns."[24]

   Blood's was a philosophy five hundred years in the making:
he gave voice to the practical idealism—pluralistic, creative,
dangerous—that had silently guided the Blood family from
its very inception. Benjamin's philosophy described a strain of
uniquely American thinking, and would resonate with a growing number of Anglo-American thinkers, such as Emerson
and James but also Josiah Royce and George Santayana, who
wanted to explore the borders of conscious life and understand
reality by way of its diversity rather than its lockstep unity. As
James struggled against the heart disease that would ultimately
kill him, he composed *The Varieties of Religious Experience* and
found comfort, once again, in Blood's mysticism, in its conclusion that, in his words, "remained unshaken": "It is that our
normal waking consciousness, rational consciousness as we call

it, is but one special type of consciousness, whilst all about it, parted from it by the filmiest of screens, there lie potential forms of consciousness entirely different."[25] Even in the face of impending darkness, there remains something new hovering on the brink of shadow, if one is willing to look into the fading light of dusk. Blood wanted his reader to come to, however briefly, and to realize that, in his words, "we are the first to dive into this silent sea." This wild possibility does not forsake us, even when we occasionally forsake it. For Blood, as for Thoreau, the vibrancy and longevity of the world depends, in no small part, on this possibility. Blood gives a reader hope and a challenge: "The 'inexplicable,' the 'mystery,' as what the intellect, with its claim to reason out reality, thinks that it is in duty bound to resolve . . . remains; but it remains as something to be met and dealt with by faculties more akin to our activities and heroisms and willingness, than to our logical powers."[26] Activity, heroism, and sheer willingness—bordering on madness—is what all the Bloods, beginning with the jewel thief Thomas, were after.

IN 1896, JAMES had written to Benjamin Blood, "I will, I promise, make you famous one day. You can count on W.J.!"[27] Thirteen years later, James entered the final season of his life and sat down at a desk in a spa in Nauheim, Germany. He had traveled there in the hope that the trip might save his life. It would not. What kept James alive, at least for the time being, was an unforgotten promise—he settled in behind his desk and began to write his final essay, titled "A Pluralistic Mystic." This was essentially a letter of farewell and thanks to Benjamin Blood, who had remained a kindred spirit for more than thirty years. It was his final attempt to make good on a commitment

THE MYSTIC   229

to this American Blood. Some promises are overlooked as death encroaches—one has time for so little at the end—but others become more pressing. James opened "A Pluralistic Mystic":

> I have always held the opinion that one of the first duties of a good reader is to summon other readers to the enjoyment of any unknown author of rare quality whom he may discover in his explorations. Now for years my own taste, literary as well as philosophic, has been exquisitely titillated by a writer the name of whom I think must be unknown to the readers of this article; so I no longer continue silent about the merits of Benjamin Paul Blood.[28]

This paean to Blood appeared after James's death in *The Hibbert Journal*, the largest and most distinguished scholarly periodical of the day, with what James called "a choice and expansive circulation of 12,000."[29] James could have written anything, or nothing at all, at the end of his days. Perhaps he felt himself to be in Blood's debt, but more likely in the sway of camaraderie, an affinity in life and thought. In the failing of his health—and the distraction that attended it—James drew heavily from Blood's writings in providing an apology for his own philosophy of action and pluralistic mysticism. *The Hibbert* was, in fact, the perfect venue for him to distill the thought of his dear American Blood: "Philosophy must pass from words, that reproduce but ancient elements, to life itself, that gives the integrally new."[30]

As he finished "A Pluralistic Mystic," James purchased one book at Nauheim in the fall of 1910: Friedrich Nietzsche's *The Birth of Tragedy*. I found this exact copy many years ago, in a New Hampshire wood, at one of the darkest moments of my life.

This book, once owned by James, is Nietzsche's first attempt to affirm human existence in the face of human frailty, fallibility, and suffering—an apt selection for a dying man. James did something he rarely would: he took his pencil and underlined one substantial passage in the book. It is the story of Nietzsche's hero Silenus, the half man, half wild beast from Greek mythology who famously suggested to King Midas that the best a person can actually do in life is to die "as quickly as possible." Life is to be lived brightly, fiercely, wildly. Nietzsche knew that there may be casualties in such a life, an acknowledgment that drew him to an ancient idea, the amor fati, or love of fate, the power to not only bear, but to hold dear, the most despicable and maddening moments of one's history. Burn quickly, brightly, for better and for worse. If this suggestion seems wild, bewildering, and heedless, perhaps one might remember that life itself is wild, bewildering, and heedless. This is the essence of Benjamin Blood's mystical revelation. At the conclusion of his review of Blood, written at the brink of death, James writes, "Mr. Blood's revelation, whatever the conditions be, helps him to stand ready for a life among them. In this, his attitude seems to resemble that of Nietzsche's *amor fati*!"

The secret of Blood's philosophy is that it's ultimately not about philosophy at all. The life of the mind is not, and will never be, life itself. And the affirmation of life, the power to embrace it even in its most tragic and wild aspects, is performed not in thinking but in living fully through to the very end. In Thoreau's words, "We are all sculptors and painters, and our material is our own flesh and blood and bone." Blood invites us into the activity of a free life, in its ongoing revolution, in the strange and miraculous space of reality. This echoes an important, if marginal, position in philosophy expressed by the eighteenth-century Scot David Hume, who instructed, "Be a philosopher, but in your philosophy be still a man."[31] This was the guiding ethos of Blood's thinking: strive to be a thoughtful human being, yet a vibrant, thriving one.

In "A Pluralistic Mystic," a dying James nearly quivers before Blood's words, writing,

> "Ever not quite!"—this seems to wring the very last panting word out [of] . . . philosophy's mouth . . . There is no complete generalization, no total point of view, no all-pervasive unity, but everywhere some residual resistance to verbalization, formulation, and discursification, some genius of reality that escapes from the pressure of the logical finger, that says "hands off," and claims its privacy, and means to be left to its own life. In every moment of immediate experience is somewhat absolutely original and novel . . . there is no conclusion . . . Farewell![32]

At the end of a life, at the end of a grand story, when it appears that there is nothing new under the sun, Blood's open "pluriverse" beckons. There is more to come. The possibilities of reality can never be fully explored and that, above all else, may be the saving grace of being human. Having reviewed Blood's pluralism in the grim twilight of his final days, James writes, "I confess that the existence of this novel brand of mysticism has made my cowering mood depart."[33]

"EVER NOT QUITE." What is the meaning of this slogan for life? Never utterly; never completely; never finished. Hopeful, urgent, frustrating, it is a phrase suited to life on the way—

provisional, partially fulfilled, almost there. It is the sense that there are lands and ideas yet to be explored, and the most honest and human endeavors are those that never fully culminate. We never succeed exactly in the ways that we expect. And this is probably for the best. It is the lingering feeling—bittersweet and tragic—that life lived at its extremity is necessarily short-lived. Ever not quite. It describes the attempts of Thomas Blood to revolt against the Crown. He very nearly got away with it. James and Thaddeus of Concord picked up where the jewel thief left off, forging the beginnings of a new nation. But just the eccentric beginnings. What began in an act of "settlement" deepened and expanded in the celestial freedoms of Perez, the recluse, and the zealous industry of Aretas, the capitalist. But then the Civil War descended, a brutal reminder that the nation was only in the making. This was the lesson that James Blood learned in Bloody Kansas, a site of destruction but also revival. In the shadow of this conflict, James Harvey Blood of St. Louis envisioned a more perfect union, one in which free love and spiritualism could grow into something real and lasting. For a time, with his wife Victoria Woodhull Blood, it lasted, until it didn't. James's idealism flared up, and out, to the end, when it silently disappeared on the coast of Africa. But something in kind was resurrected in the mystical, wide-eyed writings of Benjamin Blood—and passed on to you, in the lines of *American Bloods*. "Ever not quite"—to never fully arrive, but also, blessedly, fatefully, to never fully finish.

EPILOGUE: THE WOODS ≡≡≡

"There are two wolves," he said, "two wolves in all of us. One is good and one is evil, and they are constantly at war." His grandson nodded and cleared his throat: "Which one will win, Grandfather?" He looked down at the boy. "I am not sure, but it is said that the one who wins is the one you feed."

—AN AMERICAN LEGEND

OCTOBER 30, 1692. JOHN BLOOD, THE BROTHER TO the original settler Robert, woke before first light, gathered his coat and guns, and set out with his dogs into the Tophet Swamp abutting the Concord River. There was something wild in the cackling shadows—and John found it.

As the frost descends in New England, the swamp mud forms a seemingly stable crust that is anything but. When it gives way under a man's weight, the wet ground consumes him. John Blood went missing for eleven days. On November 11, 1692, Blood's neighbor, Thomas Sewell, wrote in his diary that Blood was "found dead in the woods, leaning his Brest on a

Logg: Had been seeking some Creatures. Oh! What strange work the Lord about to bring to Pass."

According to legend, which is what small-town rumors sometimes become, John's gun was still in his hands. Did he drown or starve? Was he attacked or mutilated? Did he have a heart attack or a stroke? It is unclear whether the gun in his hand was a rifle or a very early flintlock pistol. If it was a pistol—and that is what people still claim after more than three centuries—this gun would not have been used for hunting. This is a weapon of impulse—destructive, self-destructive, wild, like the creatures John Blood sought out.[1] He died propped against a log in the Tophet Swamp at the edge of our backyard.[2]

OCTOBER 23, 2022. Our children, like all children, frequently wake before dawn, eat breakfast as the sun rises, and want nothing more than to race outside to greet the day. And they are very fortunate, because they are still young and free and can do precisely that. Henry is five and, like Henry David Thoreau, a wild child. We can't settle him down any more than ask the wind not to blow. It was cold that morning, on the winter side of fall—late October in New England—as he took off across the frost-covered grass, away from the house that Josiah Blood built so many years ago, across the hills toward the swamp, stretching into the river below. He was told, in no uncertain terms, to go no farther than the massive white pine at the top of the gentle rise a hundred meters from the side door. As I finished the dishes at the sink, Henry's nattering slowly faded away, and I lost myself in the blessed silence of a house that had yet to fully rouse itself.

Silence in a household of children is a blessing, until it is not—then it is simply terrifying. I heard him yelling minutes before I found him. I ran to the pine and looked down into a clearing that abutted the woods. There he stood, all three and a half feet of him, in the middle of the shallow swale, calling for me at the top of his lungs. Our dog, an oversized retriever, stood next to him, rigid, pointing into the forest. Henry wasn't particularly upset, just insistent: he wanted me to see something. I joined them in the field and followed his outstretched finger with my eyes: fifty feet from him, emerging from the shadow of an ancient oak, were the shoulders and lowered head of an animal. Our dog didn't move, but let out a long, low growl. The animal peered out at him—and then at me—and held my gaze. And then it was gone with a flick of its long brown tail.

"Did you see that?" Henry whispered, still pointing to the hollow in the woods.

"Yes, Henry. I saw it," I said, looking down into his eyes, lovely, dark, and deep. "Let's all be careful. It lives in there."

NOTES

Prologue: The Wolf

1. Dante Alighieri, *Dante's "Inferno": The Indiana Critical Edition*, trans. and ed. Mark Musa (Bloomington: Indiana University Press, 1995), 20.
2. In some cases, the study of the Bloods was initiated in a family genealogy, privately published. The character studies included in *American Bloods* draw from historical documents used to occasionally corroborate *The Story of the Bloods*. In these cases, the historical documents will be provided first in endnotes, followed by the segment of the family tree, a reference to *The Story of the Bloods* followed by page number. See Roger Deane Harris, *The Story of the Bloods* (Boston: privately published, 1960), i.
3. Wilson Waters, *History of Chelmsford, Massachusetts* (Lowell, MA: printed for the town of Chelmsford by the Courier-Citizen Company, 1917), 429.
4. Quoted in William Cronon, *Changes in the Land: Indians, Colonists, and the Ecology of New England* (New York: Farrar, Straus and Giroux, 2011), 132.
5. *The Story of the Bloods*, 5.

The Thief

1. Niccolò Machiavelli, *The Prince*, trans. Peter Bondanella (Oxford: Oxford University Press, 2005), 60.
2. George Younghusband and Cyril Davenport, *The Crown Jewels of England* (London: Cassell, 1919), 55.
3. Younghusband and Davenport, 55.
4. *The Story of the Bloods*, 142. Another mention in public records with alternative date from 1342. See "16 Edward III—Part II," Public Records of Great Britain (Great Britain, 1900), 489.
5. Thomas Hobbes, *Leviathan*, ed. Richard Tuck (New York: Cambridge University Press, 1996), 88.
6. Corinne Comstock Weston and Janelle Renfrow Greenberg, *Subjects and*

Sovereigns: The Grand Controversy over Legal Sovereignty in Stuart England (New York: Cambridge University Press, 2003), 288.

7. Quoted in Charles Spencer, *Killers of the King: The Men Who Dared to Execute Charles I* (New York: Bloomsbury, 2014), 54.

8. Arthur Cross, *A History of England and Greater Britain* (New York: Macmillan, 1914), 508.

9. Philip Walsingham Sergeant, *Rogues and Scoundrels* (London: Hutchinson, 1924), 109.

10. George R. Gleig, *The Life of Oliver Cromwell* (Sandbornton, NH: Charles Lane, 1840), 169.

11. "A Soldier of Fortune: A True Story," in *Harper's Magazine,* vol. 88, 1893, 104. Also documented in outstanding detail in Robert Hutchinson, *The Audacious Crimes of Colonel Blood: The Spy Who Stole the Crown Jewels and Became the King's Secret Agent* (New York: Pegasus, 2016).

12. Quoted in Hutchinson, *The Audacious Crimes of Colonel Blood*, 25.

13. "A Soldier of Fortune," 103–5.

14. Sergeant, *Rogues and Scoundrels*, 117.

15. Sergeant, *Rogues and Scoundrels*, 117.

16. Quoted in *English Historical Documents, 1660–1714*, ed. David C. Douglas (New York: Routledge, 1996), 153.

17. Wilbur Cortez Abbott, *Colonel Thomas Blood: Crown-Stealer 1618–1680* (Rochester, NY: [Genesee Press], 1910), 96.

18. National Portrait Gallery, NPG 418.

19. Quoted in E. Beresford Chancellor, *The Private Palaces of London: Past and Present* (London: Kegan Paul, Trench, Trübner, 1908), 69.

20. Edward Walford, *Old and New London* (New York: Cassell, Petter & Galpin, 1880), 198.

21. Described in Imogen Peck, *Recollection in the Republics: Memories of the British Civil Wars in England, 1649–1659* (New York: Oxford University Press, 2021), 155.

22. There are many versions of the heist. This account has been culled from a number of sources, with a mind to the most likely events being the ones that overlap between Abbott, *Colonel Thomas Blood*; Sergeant, *Rogues and Scoundrels*; and Hutchinson, *The Audacious Crimes of Colonel Blood*.

23. John O'London's Weekly, "Robbery in the Grand Manner," *Maclean's,* April 1, 1930, 57.

24. Account detailed in "Colonel Blood" in *Kirby's Wonderful and Scientific Museum,* vol. 2 (London: R. S. Kirby, 1804), 109. This account serves as the basis for the descriptions in the most recent and authoritative ren-

dering of Thomas Blood in Hutchinson, *The Audacious Crimes of Colonel Blood*.

25. Quoted in "Colonel Blood," *Kirby's Wonderful and Scientific Museum*, 109.

26. Hutchinson, *The Audacious Crimes of Colonel Blood*, 214.

27. Hutchinson, *The Audacious Crimes of Colonel Blood*, 214.

28. Agnes Strickland, *Lives of the Queens of England, from the Norman Conquest* (London: Colburn, 1851), 457.

29. Abbott, *Colonel Thomas Blood*, 84.

30. Abbott, *Colonel Thomas Blood*, 78.

31. Abbott, *Colonel Thomas Blood*, 78.

32. Abbott, *Colonel Thomas Blood*, 88.

33. David C. Hanrahan, *Colonel Blood: The Man Who Stole the Crown Jewels* (Dublin: Sutton, 2003), 167.

34. Abbott, *Colonel Thomas Blood*, 91.

The Settlers

1. Herbert Milton Sylvester, *Indian Wars of New England*, vol. 1 (Boston: W. B. Clarke, 1910), 170.

2. Lemuel Shattuck, *A History of the Town of Concord, Middlesex County, Massachusetts from Its Earliest Settlement to 1832; and of the Adjoining Towns, Bedford, Acton, Lincoln, and Carlisle; Containing Various Notices of County and State History Not Before Published* (Boston: Russell, Odiorne, 1835), 65.

3. Shattuck, *A History of the Town of Concord*, 65.

4. Jill Lepore provides a unique and powerful interpretation of life on the American frontier of New England. For articulation of "Englishness," see Lepore, *The Name of War: King Philip's War and the Origins of American Identity* (New York: Knopf, 2009), 94.

5. Michael Parker, *John Winthrop: Founding the City Upon a Hill* (New York: Taylor and Francis, 2013), 192.

6. Parker, *John Winthrop*, 12.

7. Jeremy Black, *Crisis of Empire: Britain and America in the Eighteenth Century* (New York: Bloomsbury, 2008), 4.

8. Shattuck, *A History of the Town of Concord*, 364.

9. Shattuck, 364. Description of Robert Blood's disposition found in *The Story of the Bloods*, iv.

10. George Francis Dow, ed., *Records and Files of the Quarterly Courts of Essex County, Massachusetts*, vol. 1 (Salem, MA: Essex Institute, 1911), 133.

11. Dow, *Records and Files of the Quarterly Courts*, 133.

12. Dow, *Records and Files of the Quarterly Courts*, 133.

13. Don Gleason Hill, ed., *The Early Records of the Town of Dedham* (Dedham, MA, 1893), 238.

14. Alfred Sereno Hudson, *The History of Concord*, vol. 1 (Boston: Erudite Press, 1904), 383.

15. Hudson, *The History of Concord*, 489.

16. Annex, Gleason Public Library, Carlisle, MA. Last accessed September 2022.

17. *The Story of the Bloods*, iv.

18. Thomas Hobbes, *De Cive*, in *Three-Text Edition of Thomas Hobbes's Political Theory: "The Elements of Law," "De Cive" and "Leviathan,"* ed. Deborah Baumgold (New York: Cambridge University Press, 2017), 238.

19. Thomas Hobbes, *Leviathan; Or, The Matter, Form and Power of a Commonwealth, Ecclesiastical and Civil* (London: Routledge and Sons, 1886), 52.

20. Quoted in Christopher Edward Taucar, *The British System of Government and Its Historical Development* (Montreal: McGill-Queen's University Press, 2014), 34.

21. Henry Hazen, *History of Billerica* (Boston: Williams, 1883), 70.

22. Caleb Butler, *History of the Town of Groton* (Boston: T. R. Marvin, 1848), 16.

23. John Winthrop, *Winthrop's Journal "History of New England" 1630–1649*, vol. 2, ed. James Hosmer (New York: Scribner, 1908), 93.

24. Increase Mather, *Departing Glory: Eight Jeremiads of Increase Mather* (Delmar, NY: Scholars' Fascimiles and Reprints, 1986), 12.

25. Rebecca Fraser, *The Mayflower: The Families, the Voyage, and the Founding of America* (New York: St. Martin's Press, 2017), 292.

26. Richard M. Bayles, ed., *History of Newport County, Rhode Island. From the Year 1638 to the Year 1887, Including the Settlement of Its Towns, and Their Subsequent Progress* (New York: Preston, 1888), 212.

27. George Bodge, *Soldiers in King Philip's War; Being a Critical Account of That War, with a Concise History of the Indian Wars of New England from 1620–1677* (Boston: printed for the author, 1906), 321.

28. *The New England Historical and Genealogical Register*, vol. 53 (Boston: New England Historic Genealogical Society, 1899), 192.

29. Daniel Gookin, *An Historical Account of the Doings and Sufferings of the Christian Indians in New England in the Years 1675, 1676, 1677* (1677, repr., Cambridge, MA: American Antiquarian Society, 1836); quoted in Dennis A. Connole, *The Indians of the Nipmuck Country in Southern New England, 1630–1750* (Jefferson, NC: McFarland, 2007), 175.

30. Connole, *The Indians of the Nipmuck Country*, 175.

31. Robert Boodey Caverly, *History of the Indian Wars of New England, with Eliot the Apostle Fifty Years in the Midst of Them* (Boston: J. H. Earle, 1882), 223.

32. *Celebration of the Two Hundredth Anniversary of the Settlement of Hadley, Massachusetts, at Hadley, June 8, 1859* (Northampton, MA: Bridgman & Childs, 1859), 32.

33. Samuel Green, *Groton During the Indian Wars* (Groton, 1883), 8, 32.

34. Green, *Groton*, 8, 32.

35. "Diary of Increase Mather," in *Proceedings of the Massachusetts Historical Society*, vol. 13 (Boston: Massachusetts Historical Society, 1900), 400.

36. Franklin B. Sanborn, *Henry D. Thoreau* (Boston: Riverside Press, 1882), 214.

37. Thomas Hobbes, *The Philosophy of Hobbes in Extracts and Notes Collated from His Writings*, ed. Frederick Woodbridge (Minneapolis: H. W. Wilson, 1903), 214.

38. Hobbes, *The Philosophy of Hobbes*, 214.

39. Lepore, *The Name of War*, 94–97.

40. Increase Mather, *The History of King Philip's War* (Albany, NY: J. Munsell, 1862), 201.

41. Hobbes, *Leviathan*, 73.

42. Donald A. Lapham, *Carlisle, Composite Community* (Carlisle, MA: privately printed, 1970), 29.

43. Charles Walcott, *Concord in the Colonial Period Being a History of the Town of Concord, Massachusetts, from the Earliest Settlement to the Overthrow of the Andros Government, 1635–1689* (Boston: Estes and Lauriat, 1884), 63; *The Story of the Bloods*, 3–6.

44. *The Story of the Bloods*, 3–6.

45. *The Story of the Bloods*, 3–6.

46. *The Essex Antiquarian: A Quarterly Magazine Devoted to the Biography, Genealogy, History and Antiquities of Essex County, Massachusetts*, vol. 6 (Salem, MA: Essex Antiquarian, 1902).

47. James Andrews, ed., *Rhetoric, Religion, and the Roots of Identity in British Colonial America* (Ann Arbor: Michigan State University Press, 2007), 91–92.

48. Charles Andrews, *The American Nation: A History*, vol. 22, *National Expansion* (New York: Harper's, 1904), 277.

49. B. B. Edwards and W. Cogswell, eds., *The American Quarterly Register* (Boston: Perkins & Marvin, 1840), 116.

50. John Locke, "The Second Treatise of Civil Government," in *Two Treatises of Government*, ed. Peter Laslett (Cambridge: Cambridge University Press, 1988), 223–224.

51. Martin J. Spalding, *The History of the Protestant Reformation*, vol. 1 (New York: John Murphy, 1860), 507.

52. Locke, "The Second Treatise," 232.

53. Locke, "The Second Treatise," 222.

54. Sidney A. Bull, *History of the Town of Carlisle, Massachusetts 1754–1920* (Cambridge, MA: Murray Printing, 1920), 1–6.

55. Bull, *History of the Town of Carlisle*, 1–6.

56. Bull, *History of the Town of Carlisle*, 152.

The Minuteman

1. Ralph Waldo Emerson, "The Concord Memorial," in *Society and Solitude* (London: J. M. Dent, 1920), 162.

2. Dates of the meeting are not agreed upon. Most likely it was July 30, as per the fragment at the Concord Free Public Library. See Ralph Waldo Emerson Papers, 1835–1871, Concord Free Public Library, vault 35, unit 2.

3. Ralph Waldo Emerson, *The Complete Works of Ralph Waldo Emerson: Miscellanies*, vol. 11, ed. E. Emerson (New York: Houghton Mifflin, 1906), 565.

4. Carlisle Historical Society, *Carlisle* (Charleston, SC: Arcadia, 2005), 72.

5. Ralph Waldo Emerson Papers, 1835–1871, vault 35, unit 2; Emerson, *The Complete Works*, 565.

6. Emerson, "The Concord Memorial," 164.

7. Emerson, "The Concord Memorial," 164.

8. Emerson, "The Concord Memorial," 164.

9. Ralph Waldo Emerson Papers, 1835–1871, vault 35, unit 2.

10. Ralph Waldo Emerson Papers, 1835–1871, vault 35, unit 2.

11. *The Story of the Bloods*, 16.

12. *MHC Reconnaissance Survey Town Report: Carlisle* (Boston: Massachusetts Historical Commission, 1980), 3.

13. *MHC Town Report: Carlisle*, 3.

14. Isaiah Berlin, *Two Concepts of Liberty: An Inaugural Lecture Delivered Before the University of Oxford on 31 October 1958* (Oxford: Clarendon, 1958), 2–7.

15. Berlin, *Two Concepts of Liberty*, 2–7.

16. *The Story of the Bloods*, 16.

17. *The Story of the Bloods*, 16.

18. Wendy Warren, *New England Bound: Slavery and Colonization in Early America* (New York: Liveright, 2016).

19. Detailed discussion in Robert Bernasconi and Anika Maaza Mann, "The Contradiction of Racism," in *Race and Racism in Modern Philosophy*, ed. Andrew Valls (Ithaca, NY: Cornell University Press, 2005), 92.

20. See the definitive work of Elise Lemire, *Black Walden: Slavery and Its Aftermath in Concord, Massachusetts* (Philadelphia: University of Pennsylvania Press, 2009).

21. *The Story of the Bloods*, 16.

22. For a detailed account of the world in which the early Bloods were raised, see Robert Gross, *The Minutemen and Their World* (New York: Farrar, Straus and Giroux, 1976). Quoted in Gross, *The Minutemen*, 94.

23. Elias Nason, *A History of the Town of Dunstable, Massachusetts, from Its Earliest Settlement to the Year of Our Lord 1873* (Boston: A. Mudge, 1877), 91.

24. Nason, *A History of the Town of Dunstable*, 91. The Bloods of Groton had personal reasons to fear the Natives. James Blood (the son of Robert's brother James) was killed by the Natives on September 13, 1692, the same year of his uncle John's suicide in Carlisle. James's extended family was taken into captivity. See Duane Hurd, *History of Middlesex County, Massachusetts, with Biographical Sketches of Many of Its Pioneers and Prominent Men*, vol. 2 (Philadelphia: J. W. Lewis, 1890), 411.

25. Nason, *A History of the Town of Dunstable*, 91.

26. Thaddeus Blood, "A Minute-Man's Story of the Concord Fight," in George Varney, *The Story of Patriot's Day, Lexington and Concord, April 19, 1775, with Poems Brought Out on the First Observation of the Anniversary Holiday, and the Forms in Which It Was Celebrated* (Boston: Lee and Shepherd, 1895), 81.

27. John Adams, *The Works of John Adams*, vol. 2 (Loschberg, Germany: Jurgen Beck, reprinted 2007), 165.

28. Declaration of Rights of the Stamp Act Congress, October 19, 1765.

29. Blood, "A Minute-Man's Story," 81.

30. Theodore Draper, *A Struggle for Power: The American Revolution* (New York: Vintage, 1997), 475.

31. Preservation of documents described in Allen French, *The Day of Concord and Lexington: The Nineteenth of April, 1775* (Boston: Little, Brown, 1925), 157.

32. French, *The Day of Concord and Lexington*, 157.

33. French, *The Day of Concord and Lexington*, 157.

34. Ralph Waldo Emerson Papers, 1835–1871, vault 35, unit 2.

35. Ralph Waldo Emerson, *The Journals and Miscellaneous Notebooks of Ralph Waldo Emerson* (Cambridge, MA: Belknap Press, 1966), 242.

36. Emerson, *The Journals and Miscellaneous Notebooks*, 242.

37. Emerson, *The Journals and Miscellaneous Notebooks*, 242.

38. Emerson, *The Journals and Miscellaneous Notebooks*, 242.

39. Emerson, *The Journals and Miscellaneous Notebooks*, 242.

40. Detailed by Emerson in his *The Complete Works*, 74.

41. Emerson, "The Concord Memorial," 162.

42. Emerson, "The Concord Memorial," 162.

43. In Robert D. Richardson Jr., *Emerson: The Mind on Fire* (Berkeley: University of California Press, 1995), 25.

44. Blood, "A Minute-Man's Story," 81.

45. Ralph Waldo Emerson, "The American Scholar," in *The Collected Works of Ralph Waldo Emerson: Nature, Addresses, and Lectures*, vol. 1 (Cambridge, MA: Belknap Press, 1971), 59.

46. Emerson, "The American Scholar," 89.

47. Ralph Waldo Emerson, *Journals of Ralph Waldo Emerson*, vol. 6, ed. E. Emerson (Boston: Houghton Mifflin, 1909), 36.

48. Mason I. Lowance Jr., ed., *A House Divided: The Antebellum Slavery Debates in America, 1776–1865* (Princeton, NJ: Princeton University Press, 2003), 206.

49. Lowance, *A House Divided*, 206.

50. Emerson, *The Complete Works*, 111.

51. Quoted in Jennifer Putzi, *Identifying Marks: Race, Gender, and the Marked Body in Nineteenth-Century America* (Athens: University of Georgia Press, 2006), 108.

52. Emerson, *The Complete Works*, 115.

53. Emerson, *The Complete Works*, 115.

The Stargazer

1. Henry David Thoreau, *The Writings of Henry David Thoreau. Journal*, vol. 8 (Boston: Houghton Mifflin, 1906), 151.

2. Hudson, *The History of Concord*, 43.

3. George Tolman, *Concord, Massachusetts Births, Marriages, and Deaths, 1635–1850* (Boston: Beacon Press, 1895), 261.

4. William Ellery Channing, "The Barren Moors," in *American Poetry: The Nineteenth Century*, vol. 2, ed. John Hollander (New York: Taylor and Francis, 2016), 674.

5. Kenneth Cameron, ed., *The Massachusetts Lyceum During the American Renaissance. Materials for the Study of the Oral Tradition in American Letters: Emerson, Thoreau, Hawthorne, and Other New-England Lecturers* (Hartford, CT: Transcendental Books, 1969), 34.

6. My understanding of Emerson and Thoreau was shaped and is buttressed by the magisterial works of Robert Richardson. For an account of astronomy in Thoreau, see Richardson, *Henry Thoreau: A Life of the Mind* (Berkeley: University of California Press, 1988), 184.

7. Henry David Thoreau, *Walden* (Cambridge: Crowell, 1910), 119.

8. Richardson, *Henry Thoreau*, 175–180.

9. A beautiful explication of this comment is found in Stanley Cavell, *The Senses of Walden: An Expanded Edition* (Chicago: University of Chicago Press, 1972), 52.

10. Next to Richardson, Laura Dassow Walls's work on Thoreau remains unparalleled. For a detailed description of Thoreau's relationship with Lidian Emerson, see Walls, *Henry David Thoreau: A Life* (Chicago: University of Chicago Press, 2017), 231–239.

11. Henry David Thoreau, "The Emerson–Thoreau Correspondence," *Atlantic Monthly*, vol. 69, 1892, 737.

12. Ralph Waldo Emerson Papers, 1835–1871, Concord Free Public Library, vault 35, unit 3.

13. Henry David Thoreau, *The Writings of Henry David Thoreau*, vol. 6 (Boston: Houghton Mifflin, 1906), 134.

14. Thoreau, *The Writings of Henry David Thoreau*, vol. 6, 137.

15. Thoreau, *The Writings of Henry David Thoreau*, 137.

16. Henry David Thoreau, *"Walden," "Civil Disobedience," and Other Writings* (New York: W. W. Norton, 2008), 230.

17. Thoreau, *"Walden," "Civil Disobedience," and Other Writings*, 229.

18. Henry David Thoreau, *The Writings of Henry David Thoreau. Journal*, vol. 3 (Boston: Houghton Mifflin, 1906), 10.

19. Thoreau, *The Writings of Henry David Thoreau. Journal*, vol. 3, 10.

20. Thoreau, *The Writings of Henry David Thoreau. Journal*, vol. 3, 10.

21. Henry David Thoreau, *The Writings of Henry David Thoreau. Journal*, vol. 2 (Boston: Houghton Mifflin, 1906), 288.

22. Thoreau, *The Writings of Henry David Thoreau. Journal*, vol. 2, 288.

23. Thoreau, *The Writings of Henry David Thoreau. Journal*, vol. 2, 288.

24. Henry David Thoreau, *"Wild Fruits": Thoreau's Rediscovered Last Manuscript* (New York: W. W. Norton, 2001), 367.

25. Thoreau, *The Writings of Henry David Thoreau. Journal*, vol. 2, 288.

26. Thoreau, *The Writings of Henry David Thoreau. Journal*, vol. 5 (Boston: Houghton Mifflin, 1906), 410.

27. Kevin Dann provides a detailed description of Thoreau's astrological interests and an interesting interpretation of this passage. Quoted in Dann, *Expect Great Things: The Life and Search of Henry David Thoreau* (New York: TarcherPerigee, 2017), 225.

28. Walter Harding, *The Days of Henry David Thoreau: A Biography* (Princeton, NJ: Princeton University Press, 1982), 224.

29. Henry David Thoreau, *The Writings of Henry David Thoreau. Journal*, vol. 9 (Boston: Houghton Mifflin, 1906), 137.

30. Thoreau, *The Writings of Henry David Thoreau. Journal*, vol. 9, 137.

31. Thoreau, *The Writings of Henry David Thoreau. Journal*, vol. 9, 83.

32. Thoreau, *"Walden," "Civil Disobedience," and Other Writings*, 220.

33. Richardson, *Henry Thoreau*, 153.

34. Thoreau, *The Writings of Henry David Thoreau. Journal*, vol. 8, 151.

35. Thoreau, *Walking* (Cambridge, MA: Riverside Press, 1914), 3.

36. Quoted in and explained by Walls, *Henry David Thoreau: A Life*, 286.

37. Thoreau, *"Wild Fruits": Thoreau's Rediscovered Last Manuscript*, 25.

38. Henry David Thoreau, *The Writings of Henry David Thoreau. Journal*, vol. 12 (Boston: Houghton Mifflin, 1906), 348.

39. A beautiful rendering of this comment is given in Richard Higgins, *Thoreau and the Language of Trees* (Berkeley: University of California Press, 2017), 58.

40. Higgins, *Thoreau and the Language of Trees*, 58.

41. Henry David Thoreau, *The Writings of Henry David Thoreau. Journal*, vol. 14 (Boston: Houghton Mifflin, 1906), 362.

42. Samuel Drake, *History of Middlesex County, Massachusetts, Containing Carefully Prepared Histories of Every City and Town in the County*, vol. 1 (Boston: Estes and Lauriat, 1880), 403.

43. Duane Hurd, *History of Middlesex County, Massachusetts, with Biographical Sketches of Many of Its Pioneers and Prominent Men*, vol. 2 (Philadelphia: J. W. Lewis, 1890), 602.

The Machinist

1. There are a variety of references, but see an early use in Johann Ebers, *Vollständiges Wörterbuch der Englischen Sprache für die Deutschen* (*The New and Complete Dictionary of the German and English Languages*), vol. 5 (Leipzig: Breitkopf and Hertzel, 1799), 905.

2. William K. Klingaman and Nicholas P. Klingaman, *The Year Without a*

Summer: 1816 and the Volcano That Darkened the World and Changed History (New York: St. Martin's Press, 2014).

3. Klingaman and Klingaman, *The Year Without a Summer*, 56–57.

4. Quoted in Klingaman and Klingaman, *The Year Without a Summer*, 195.

5. Samuel Goodrich, *Peter Parley's Own Story. From the Personal Narrative of the Late Samuel G. Goodrich ("Peter Parley")* (New York: Sheldon, 1864), 155.

6. "Aretas Blood," *Granite Monthly*, vol. 10, March 1887, 81–86.

7. Quoted in Klingaman and Klingaman, *The Year Without a Summer*, 46.

8. "Aretas Blood," in *Memorial Encyclopedia of the State of New Hampshire*, ed. James A. Ellis (New York: American Historical Society, 1919), 27.

9. "Aretas Blood," in *Memorial Encyclopedia of the State of New Hampshire*, 27.

10. Henry David Thoreau, "To Mr. B," in *Letters to Various Persons* (Boston: Ticknor and Fields, 1865), 161.

11. Quoted in William Pole, *The Life of Robert Stephenson, F.R.S., with Descriptive Chapters on Some of His Most Important Professional Works* (Cambridge: Cambridge University Press, 2014 [1868]), 124.

12. Quoted in Frederick McDermott, "Some Features of Railway Travel, Past and Present," *Journal of the Society of Arts* 49, no. 2519 (March 1901): 223.

13. McDermott, "Some Features of Railway Travel," 223.

14. This description of the "iron horse" in relation to Aretas was initiated in *The Story of the Bloods*, 52. For Smith poem, see Samuel Smith, "Locomotives," in *Miscellaneous Writings of the Late Samuel J. Smith, of Burlington, N.J.* (Philadelphia: Perkins, 1836), 213.

15. William Brown, *The History of the First Locomotives in America. From Original Documents, and the Testimony of Living Witnesses* (New York: Appleton, 1871), 87.

16. "Aretas Blood," *Granite Monthly*, 82.

17. A compelling interpretation of this passage is given in Tom Brass, "Capitalism, Primitive Accumulation and Unfree Labour," in *Imperialism, Crisis and Class Struggle: The Enduring Verities and Contemporary Face of Capitalism*, ed. Henry Veltmeyer (New York: Brill, 2010), 72.

18. Brass, "Capitalism," 72.

19. Karl Marx, *The Collected Works of Karl Marx*, vol. 4 (London: Lawrence and Wishert, 1975), 277.

20. Karl Marx, *The Essential Marx*, ed. Leon Trotsky (New York: Dover, 2006), 174.

21. Karl Marx, *Capital*, vol. 1 (New York: Penguin, 2004), 87.

22. Marx, *Capital*, vol. 1, 233.

23. "Aretas Blood," *Granite Monthly*, 83.

24. Watt and Wilkinson are described in various sources. See an early account in "The Founder of the Iron Trade," *The Builder*, October 16, 1886, 552–555.

25. Frank M. Gilbert, *History of the City of Evansville and Vanderburg County, Indiana*, vol. 1 (Evansville, IN: Tri-State Genealogical Society, 1988), 49.

26. Gilbert, *History of the City of Evansville*, 49.

27. John H. White Jr., *A History of the American Locomotive: Its Development, 1830–1880* (New York: Dover, 1979), 450.

28. Lowell Historical Society, *Lowell: The River City* (Charleston, SC: Arcadia, 2006), 136.

29. Quoted and discussed in Richard J. Schneider, *Civilizing Thoreau: Human Ecology and the Emerging Social Sciences in the Major Works* (Rochester, NY: Camden House, 2006), 112.

30. Charles Dickens, "The Wholesome Factory," in *American Notes, and Reprinted Pieces*, vol. 4 (London: Chapman & Hall, 1868), 42.

31. John White, *A History of the American Locomotive*, 450.

32. White, *A History of the American Locomotive*, 451.

33. "Aretas Blood," *Memorial Encyclopedia of the State of New Hampshire*, 29.

34. "Aretas Blood," *Memorial Encyclopedia of the State of New Hampshire*, 29.

35. "Aretas Blood," *Memorial Encyclopedia of the State of New Hampshire*, 29.

36. "Aretas Blood," *Memorial Encyclopedia of the State of New Hampshire*, 29.

37. "Aretas Blood," *Memorial Encyclopedia of the State of New Hampshire*, 29.

38. Frank Taussig, *Principles of Economics*, vol. 1 (New York: Macmillan, 1919), 41.

39. Critical commentary of Gast's work can be found in Amy Greenberg, *Manifest Manhood and the Antebellum American Empire* (New York: Cambridge University Press, 2005), 1–3.

40. Cihan Bilginsoy, *A History of Financial Crises: Dreams and Follies of Expectations* (New York: Taylor and Francis, 2014), 188.

41. Robert B. Perreault, *Manchester* (Charleston, SC: Arcadia, 2005), 22.

42. Henry David Thoreau, *"Walden," "Civil Disobedience," and Other Writings* (New York: W. W. Norton, 2008), 183.

43. Ralph Waldo Emerson, *The Journals and Miscellaneous Notebooks of Ralph Waldo Emerson*, vol. 11, *1848–1851*, ed. A. W. Plumstead and William Gilman (Cambridge, MA: Belknap Press, 1975), 75.

44. Emerson, *The Journals and Miscellaneous Notebooks*, 71.

45. Quoted in *Popular Mechanics: An Illustrated Weekly Review of the Mechanical Press of the World*, vol. 16, 1911, 308.

46. Quoted in the transcendentalist *Dial*, the principal platform of Thoreau, Emerson, and Fuller in the first half of the nineteenth century. Translated in the later reviving of *The Dial* from the third German edition of Marx's *Capital* by Arthur Woodford, "Scientific Socialism," *The Dial*, vol. 9, March 1889, 282.

47. The Locomotive Club, "History of the Manchester Works of the American Locomotive Co.," *Loco*, vol. 12–13, 1910, 7.

48. "Aretas Blood," *Granite Monthly*, 82.

49. "Aretas Blood," *Memorial Encyclopedia of the State of New Hampshire*, 31.

50. Jane Addams, *Democracy and Social Ethics* (New York: Macmillan, 1902), 16.

51. Friedrich Engels, "Barbarous Indifference," in *The Many Faces of Evil: Historical Perspectives*, ed. Amélie Oksenberg Rorty (New York: Routledge, 2001), 251.

52. John Moore, *Columbia and Richland County: A South Carolina Community, 1740–1990* (Columbia: University of South Carolina Press, 1993), 304.

53. Moore, *Columbia and Richland County*, 304.

54. Trudy Irene Scee, *Garden Cemeteries of New England* (Lanham, MD: Down East Books, 2019), 66–67.

55. Moore, *Columbia and Richland County*, 403.

The Survivor

1. John James Audubon, "The Missouri River Journals," in *Audubon and His Journals*, vol. 2, ed. Maria R. Audubon (New York: Charles Scribner's Sons, 1897), 67.

2. *The Story of the Bloods*, 64–66.

3. William E. Unrau, *The Rise and Fall of Indian Country, 1825–1855* (Lawrence: University of Kansas Press, 2007), 53.

4. *The Story of the Bloods*, 64.

5. Adam Wesley Dean, *An Agrarian Republic: Farming, Antislavery Politics, and Nature Parks in the Civil War Era* (Chapel Hill: University of North Carolina Press, 2015), 45.

6. Dean, *An Agrarian Republic*, 45.

7. Charles Robinson, *The Kansas Conflict* (New York: Harper and Brothers, 1892), 184.

8. *The Story of the Bloods*, 65.

9. Oswald Garrison Villard, *John Brown, 1800–1859: A Biography Fifty Years After* (Boston: Houghton Mifflin, 1911), 146.

10. Villard, *John Brown*, 154.

11. Quoted and placed in context in James Redpath, *Echoes of Harper's Ferry* (Boston: Thayer and Eldridge, 1860), 69.

12. In Frederick Douglass Papers: Speech, Article, and Book File, 1846–1894; Speeches and Articles by Douglass, 1846–1894; 1860; "A Lecture on John Brown," 1–35, Library of Congress, https://www.loc.gov/resource/mss11879.22002.

13. Henry David Thoreau, *The Writings of Henry David Thoreau. Journal*, vol. 10 (Boston: Houghton Mifflin, 1906), 198.

14. Frank Gent et al., *Report on Tracing the Blood Creek Community*, Chapman Center for Rural Studies, August 2012, https://ccrsresearchcollections.omeka.net/items/show/90.

15. George W. Hunt and C. Stearns to Blood, Hutchinson, et al., Papers of the Kansas Historical Society, James Blood Collection, 281, box 1, folder 1.

16. George W. Hunt and C. Stearns to Blood, Hutchinson, et al.

17. George W. Hunt and C. Stearns to Blood, Hutchinson, et al.

18. C. W. Holder to James Blood, Papers of the Kansas Historical Society, James Blood Collection, 281, box 1, folder 1.

19. Abraham Lincoln, "Speech at Leavenworth Kansas," in *Collected Works of Abraham Lincoln* (New Brunswick, NJ: Rutgers University Press, 1953), 498.

20. Lincoln, "Speech at Leavenworth Kansas," 503.

21. William E. Connelley, *A Standard History of Kansas and Kansans*, vol. 2 (New York: Lewis Publishing, 1919), 717.

22. In an account from P. S. Sanderson in *The War of the Rebellion. A Compilation of Official Records of the Union and Confederate Armies*, series 1, vol. 2 (Washington, DC: Government Printing Office, 1894), 107.

23. William Baxter, *Pea Ridge and Prairie Grove: Or, Scenes and Incidents of the War in Arkansas* (New York: Carlton & Lanahan, 1864), 88.

24. Duane Schultz, *Quantrill's War: The Life and Times of William Clarke Quantrill, 1837–1865* (New York: St. Martin's Press, 1997), 150.

25. Schultz, *Quantrill's War*, 10.

26. Schultz, *Quantrill's War*, 11.

27. Schultz, *Quantrill's War*, 143.

28. Schultz, *Quantrill's War*, 143.

29. Peter Koch, "Life at Muscleshell in 1869 and 1870," in *Contributions to*

the Historical Society of Montana, vol. 2 (Helena, MT: State Publishing, 1896), 301.

30. William Connelley, *Quantrill and the Border Wars* (Cedar Rapids, IA: Torch Press, 1909), 349.

31. Connelley, *Quantrill and the Border Wars*, 349.

32. Connelley, *Quantrill and the Border Wars*, 378.

33. Connelley, *Quantrill and the Border Wars*, 378.

34. Jacki Thompson Rand, *Kiowa Humanity and the Invasion of the State* (Lincoln: University of Nebraska Press, 2008), 13.

35. *Senate Documents, Otherwise Publ. as Public Documents and Executive Documents: 14th Congress, 1st Session–48th Congress, 2nd Session and Special Session*, vol. 1 (Washington, DC: Government Printing Office, 1867), 121.

36. This account of Native resistance is given in Dee Brown, *Bury My Heart at Wounded Knee: An Indian History of the American West* (New York: Henry Holt, 1970), 158.

37. Henry M. Stanley, *My Early Travels and Adventures in America and Asia*, vol. 1 (London: Sampson, Low, Marston, 1895), 32.

38. Brown, *Bury My Heart at Wounded Knee*, 241.

39. Brown, *Bury My Heart at Wounded Knee*, 248.

40. Brown, *Bury My Heart at Wounded Knee*, 268–270.

41. Brown, *Bury My Heart at Wounded Knee*, 271.

42. Rebecca Onion, "The Sad History of the Kid-Sized Handcuffs," *Slate*, January 11, 2013, https://slate.com/human-interest/2013/01/small -handcuffs-the-artifact-was-used-to-bring-native-american-children-to -boarding-school.html.

The Lovers

1. Quoted in *The Awarding of the Medal of Honor to Theodore Roosevelt: Hearing Before the Military Personnel Subcommittee of the Committee on National Security, House of Representatives, One Hundred Fifth Congress, Second Session, Hearing Held September 28, 1998*, vol. 4 (Washington, DC: Government Printing Office, 1998), 87.

2. Barbara A. White, *The Beecher Sisters* (New Haven, CT: Yale University Press, 2008), 188.

3. Barbara Goldsmith, *Other Powers: The Age of Suffrage, Spiritualism, and the Scandalous Victoria Woodhull* (New York: Knopf, 2011), 201.

4. Miriam Brody, *Victoria Woodhull: Free Spirit for Women's Rights* (New York: Oxford University Press, 2011), 9.

5. Brody, *Victoria Woodhull*, 12.

6. Theodore Tilton, *A Biography of Victoria C. Woodhull* (New York: Golden Age Press, 1871), 14.

7. Tilton, *A Biography of Victoria C. Woodhull*, 14.

8. Tilton, *A Biography of Victoria C. Woodhull*, 24.

9. Barbara Goldsmith, *Other Powers*, 68.

10. Goldsmith, *Other Powers*, 68.

11. Charles Fourier, "On the Condition of Women," in *Selections from the Works of Fourier*, trans. Julia Franklin (London: Swan Sonnenschein, 1901), 76–77.

12. Fourier, "On the Condition of Women," 76–77.

13. Emanuel Swedenborg, "Heaven and Hell," in *Introducing the New Jerusalem*, trans. John Chadwick (repr., London: Swedenborg Society, 2006), 77.

14. Tilton provides a useful character study of James Blood: "philosophical, reflective, recluse from society" and a "fervent believer" in Woodhull's future. See Tilton, *A Biography of Victoria Woodhull*, 24–25.

15. Lois Beachy Underhill, *The Woman Who Ran for President: The Many Lives of Victoria Woodhull* (New York: Bridge Works, 1995), 60.

16. "Bewitching Brokers," cartoon, in *Harper's Magazine*, vol. 17, 1870, 160.

17. *Woodhull & Claflin's Weekly: The Lives and Writings of Notorious Victoria Woodhull and Her Sister Tennessee Claflin*, ed. Arlene Kisner (New York: Time Change Press, 1972), 55.

18. Victoria Claflin Woodhull, "Constitutional Equality," in *The Human Body the Temple of God; Or, the Philosophy of Sociology* (London: Hyde Park Gate, 1890), 147.

19. S. E. Schlosser, "The Tale of Elvira Blood," in *Spooky New England: Tales of Hauntings, Strange Happenings, and Other Local Lore* (Guilford, CT: Globe Pequot, 2017), 27.

20. Goldsmith, *Other Powers*, 211.

21. Goldsmith, *Other Powers*, 367.

22. Goldsmith, *Other Powers*, 367.

The Mystic

1. "William James to Alexander," in *The Letters of William James*, vol. 2 (Boston: Atlantic Monthly Press, 1920), 82.

2. Henry David Thoreau, *"Walden," "Civil Disobedience," and Other Writings* (New York: W. W. Norton, 2008), 414.

3. Benjamin Paul Blood, *The Anaesthetic Revelation and the Gist of Philosophy* (Amsterdam, NY: [s.n.], 1874), 3.

4. Ralph Waldo Emerson, "To William Emerson," in *The Letters of Ralph Waldo Emerson*, vol. 4 (New York: Columbia University Press, 1936), 479.

5. Benjamin Blood, *The Bride of the Iconoclast* (Boston: James Munroe, 1854), 32.

6. Blood, *The Bride of the Iconoclast*, 4.

7. Blood, *The Bride of the Iconoclast*, 4.

8. Blood, *The Bride of the Iconoclast*, 32.

9. William James, review of *The Anaesthetic Revelation and the Gist of Philosophy*, *Atlantic Monthly*, November 1874, https://www.theatlantic.com/past/docs/issues/96may/nitrous/wmjgist.htm.

10. James, review of *The Anaesthetic Revelation and the Gist of Philosophy*.

11. James, review *of The Anaesthetic Revelation and the Gist of Philosophy*.

12. Thoreau, *"Walden," "Civil Disobedience," and Other Writings*, 222.

13. It is no overstatement to suggest that the thought of Benjamin Blood was in the background of James's most famous essays. For example, this quotation from *The Anaesthetic Revelation* is footnoted at length in James's 1879 "Sentiment of Rationality." Quotation in Blood, *The Anaesthetic Revelation and the Gist of Philosophy*, 34.

14. William James, "Letter to Benjamin Blood," in *The Letters of William James*, vol. 2, 58.

15. Alfred, Lord Tennyson, "Letter to Benjamin Blood," in *The Letters of Alfred Lord Tennyson*, vol. 2, *1871–1892*, ed. Cecil Y. Lang and Edgar F. Shannon Jr. (Cambridge, MA: Belknap Press, 1990), 82.

16. Tennyson, "Letter to Benjamin Blood," 82.

17. Described in wonderful detail in Robert D. Richardson, *William James: In the Maelstrom of American Modernism* (New York: Houghton Mifflin Harcourt, 2006), 158.

18. James, "Letter to Benjamin Blood," 58.

19. James, "Letter to Benjamin Blood," 58.

20. Richardson, *William James*, 364.

21. Richardson, *William James*, 364.

22. Quoted in William James, "The Pluralistic Mystic," in *Hibbert Journal*, vol. 8, 1910, 756.

23. James, "Letter to Benjamin Blood," 241.

24. Quoted in Ralph Barton Perry, *The Thought and Character of William James, as Revealed in Unpublished Correspondence and Notes*, vol. 2 (Boston: Little, Brown, 1935), 233.

25. William James, "The Varieties of Religious Experience," in *William*

James: Writings 1902–1910, ed. Bruce Kuklick (New York: Library of America, 1987), 349.

26. Quoted in James, "A Pluralistic Mystic," 768.
27. James, "Letter to Benjamin Blood," 39.
28. James, "A Pluralistic Mystic," 756.
29. James, "A Pluralistic Mystic," 348.
30. James, "A Pluralistic Mystic," 348.
31. James, "A Pluralistic Mystic," 348.
32. James, "A Pluralistic Mystic," 764.
33. James, "A Pluralistic Mystic," 758.

Epilogue: The Woods
1. *The Story of the Bloods*, 4.
2. *The Story of the Bloods*, 11.

ACKNOWLEDGMENTS

This book, more than any other intellectual project I've under-taken, rests on the efforts of others. I would like to acknowl-edge the painstaking research in a variety of fields—from the preservation of tax codes and deeds by New England town clerks, to the documentation of the economics of life on Blood Farm, to the critical appraisal of the treatment of Indigenous people in the nineteenth century—that made the writing of *American Bloods* possible. Of course, all writers stand on the shoulders of giants, but I have, to this point, failed to realize how strong and how enabling these shoulders always are. I would like to thank my editor at Farrar, Straus and Giroux, Ileene Smith, who encouraged me to write *American Philosophy: A Love Story*, *Hiking with Nietzsche: On Becoming Who You Are*, and now *American Bloods*. Her creative sensibilities and keen eyes were, as always, indispensable in the course of the five-year in-vestigation of the Bloods and American wildness. Markus Hoff-man, my agent and the first reader of the manuscript, urged me on as I stumbled through unfamiliar historical territory, and forced me to take seriously Benjamin Blood's idea that life is never simply reducible to the life of the mind. Jonathan van

Belle, Douglas Anderson, Clancy Martin, and Andrea Wulf
were early readers of the manuscript and provided guidance
and invaluable suggestions. John Troast of the Carlisle Historical Society, who I am sure will write wonderful history books
in the future, also reviewed the manuscript and offered sage
advice regarding Concord and Carlisle history as well as the
Blood family genealogy.

I cannot thank my wife, Kathleen Kaag, enough. But I will
try. Thank you for walking with me through what were the most
difficult years of my life. I love you as I have loved no other. You
have taught me—by showing me—what William James meant
in his instruction "Be not afraid of life." And this line of thought
became a powerful current in *American Bloods*. Our Blood house,
seated on the Concord River, is, and will remain, a wild one:
filled with two-legged and four-legged beasts. Becca, Henry,
Lily, Mogli, Seymour: I thank you from the bottom of my heart
for helping to make my life worth living.

And I thank the wolf of Wolf Rock.

INDEX

Page numbers in *italics* refer to illustrations.

Illustration Credits

p. 13: Frederic Remington, *Moonlight, Wolf,* 1904: Addison Gallery of American Art

p. 19: The British Crown Jewels: *Illustrated Magazine,* December 13, 1952

p. 30: Gilbert Soest, *Unknown Man, Formerly Known as Thomas Blood*: National Portrait Gallery, London

p. 45: Native American communities of New England circa 1680: Nikater / Wikimedia Commons

p. 63: Map of Concord, Massachusetts: Boston Public Library, Norman B. Leventhal Map Center

p. 72: British March, April 19, 1775: "A View of the Town of Concord." Plate II Amos Doolittle, 1775 (Albany Institute of History & Art, gift, 1920)

p. 79: Ralph Waldo Emerson by Josiah Johnson Hawes 1857: Concord Free Library

p. 112: Henry David Thoreau by Benjamin D. Maxham: Concord Free Library

p. 140: Aretas Blood: Manchester Historical Society

p. 170: James Blood of Lawrence, Kansas: Kansas State Historical Society

p. 174: John Brown: Daguerreotype by John Bowles c. 1856 (Boston Athenaeum)

p. 183: Quantrill's raid of Lawrence: *Harper's Weekly* on September 5, 1863

p. 184: Massachusetts Street, Lawrence, Kansas, circa 1856: Kansas State Historical Society

p. 195: James Blood, husband of Victoria Woodhull: Missouri History Museum

p. 203: Victoria Woodhull: Fine Arts Library, Harvard University, by way of the Smithsonian Institution

p. 210: Victoria Woodhull before the Senate committee: Judiciary Committee of the U.S. House of Representatives on January 11, 1871, *Frank Leslie's Illustrated Newspaper*

p. 216: William James: Houghton Library, Harvard University

p. 216: Benjamin Paul Blood: Houghton Library, Harvard University

A Note About the Author

John Kaag is the Donahue Professor of the Arts at the University of Massachusetts, Lowell, and an external professor at the Santa Fe Institute. He is the author of *American Philosophy: A Love Story* and *Hiking with Nietzsche*, both of which were named best books of the year by NPR. His writing has appeared in *The New York Times*, *Harper's Magazine*, *The Christian Science Monitor*, and many other publications. He lives outside Boston with his wife and children.